The Psychology of the Extreme is psychology at its best—where it is supremely relevant to everyone's daily life and grounded in impeccable science yet written in a way that any layperson can understand, relate to, and appreciate. The book shows that extremism is becoming more common as the pressures of everyday life increase, but that extremism can be a virtue (e.g., Gandhi) as well as a vice (e.g., Bin Laden). No one will read this book without their life being touched by it. It is destined quickly to become a psychology classic. The book will help everyone understand the puzzling spread of extremism in today's world. I recommend the book most highly.

Robert J. Sternberg, *Professor, College of Human Ecology, Cornell University,*
Honorary Professor of Psychology, University of Heidelberg, Germany

In this book, two of America's foremost experts on terrorism explain that extremism – and the quest for significance that drives it – can motivate both world-changing scientific discoveries and artistic achievement, but also barbarism, terrorism and war. Extremists' single-minded commitment to pursuing their goals always comes at a price, whether the objective is national liberation or terrorism. These goals would often be more easily achieved, the authors counsel, through more temperate means. A fascinating, readable study on the roots of extremism, this book is medicine for a polarized age.

Jessica Stern, *Author of Terror in the Name of God, Research Professor at Boston University*

Kruglanski & Moskalenko have drawn on their substantial scientific reputation as leading scholars of extremism to deliver a true tour de force – a wide-ranging and highly engaging account of the psychological roots of extremism. Their key premise is that extremists, for good or bad, have a single-minded focus on and unwavering commitment to one dominant need and associated goals and actions, to the exclusion of all other concerns. We can all be prone to this single-mindedness, but in its more extreme form there is a high societal and personal price to such motivational selectivity and imbalance.

Michael A. Hogg, *PhD, FBA, FASSA, Professor of Social Psychology, Director, Social Identity*
Lab, President-elect, International Society for Self and Identity, Editor-in-Chief, Group Processes
and Intergroup Relations, Department of Psychology, Claremont Graduate University

Extremism is one of the most important social phenomena that we face today. In this book, Professors Arie Kruglanski and Sophia Moskalenko present a novel and coherent analysis of the determinants and consequences of extremism. Interestingly,

T0334219

they make the convincing case that extremism has both a downside and an upside and suggest ways to cultivate the latter and prevent the former. This book is a must read! I recommend it for all those interested in finding more about extremism and the crucial role it plays in everyday life.

Robert J. Vallerand, Ph.D., Author of the award-winning book, The Psychology of
Passion: A Dualistic Model, Canada Research Chair on Motivational Processes and
Optimal Functioning, Professor of Social Psychology, Université du Québec à Montréal,
Former President of the International Positive Psychology Association

From a robust basis of the importance of human goals, this book discusses both the toxic and benevolent aspects of what extremists think, feel, and do. Written in an engaging style, with lots of examples of lives well-known and lesser known, this comprehensive account of one-track-mindedness explains why extremism is both rare and can be tempting to all of us. A very important accomplishment, highly recommended for everyone interested in destructive and constructive forms of human behavior.

Kees van den Bos, Professor of Social Psychology, Professor of
Empirical Legal Science, Utrecht University

We live in an Age of Extremism. To manage, mitigate and redirect extremism, world authorities on the "Psychology of Extremism," Arie W Kruglanski and Sophia Moskalenko have authored a tour de force. After investigating the common psychology driving extremisms of all types, they develop a protocol for altering destructive extremism and reining it in. A truly innovative contribution on one of the defining issues of our times.

Prof. Rohan Gunaratna, Author of the International Bestseller,
"Inside Al Qaeda: Global Network of Terrorism"

You might think Osama Bin Laden and Mahatma Gandhi had little in common, apart from Asian birth, or Van Gogh and Madame Curie, except for years in France; and even less alike would seem the self-sacrificing abolitionist Harriet Tubman and Julius Caesar, the aggressive subjugator. But the The Psychology of the Extreme reveals through a clever and spirited blend of scientific evidence, legends from the past, and personal anecdote that all these people, and others whom history remembers most and who drive much of today's politics and creative industries, basically possess one-track personalities where "passion or idée fixe dominates the person's concerns to the exclusion of nearly all else." Whether a passion is rooted in personal ambition or reverence for humanity, or an idea is devoted to mass murder or novel knowledge, at play is the same psychological dynamic ratcheting up the Darwinian impulse to thrive. Caution and caveat are cast aside, norms and risks suppressed in a quest for significance: be it for good or ill, for peace or war, in the hunt for fulfillment in science or sport, in art or craft, in love or worship, in internet addiction or fidelity to conspiracy theory – or in the authors' own avowedly single-minded chase to understand a world "in overdrive" through academic pursuit of psychology. The book even provides readers a verbal scale to judge any proclivity of their own towards extremism, as well as practical ways to insinuate into extremism salutary moderation and wider regard for others.

Scott Atran, Emeritus Director of Research in Anthropology at the Centre national de la recherche scientifique in Paris, Research Professor at the University of Michigan, cofounder of ARTIS International and of the Centre for the Resolution of Intractable Conflict at Oxford University.

THE PSYCHOLOGY OF THE EXTREME

What does extremism mean? How does it show up in our daily lives? What drives people to extreme behaviors, and how can we learn to live and thrive in the age of overdrive?

The Psychology of the Extreme provides an accessible introduction to extremism as a force that can affect all aspects of culture and people's choices in everyday settings. It explores the underlying psychology behind what makes people act in extreme ways, whether this is in destructive ways (such as gambling, terrorism, and political violence) or in constructive ways (such as successful creators and scientists). The book features an array of case studies that show how extremism can be both pro-social and anti-social and includes interventions to reduce extremism or redirect them toward more positive and constructive tendencies. Offering a new understanding of the individual psychology of extremism, the book will appeal to all those interested in how extremism plays out in people's and cultures' day-to-day lives.

Arie W. Kruglanski is Distinguished University Professor of Psychology at the University of Maryland and a co-founding PI at START, the national center of excellence for the study of terrorism and the response to terrorism.

Sophia Moskalenko is a Research Fellow at Georgia State University and a Program Management Specialist at the UN Office of Counter Terrorism, Behavioral Insights Hub.

THE PSYCHOLOGY OF EVERYTHING

People are fascinated by psychology, and what makes humans tick. Why do we think and behave the way we do? We've all met armchair psychologists claiming to have the answers, and people that ask if psychologists can tell what they're thinking. *The Psychology of Everything* is a series of books which debunk the popular myths and pseudo-science surrounding some of life's biggest questions.

The series explores the hidden psychological factors that drive us, from our subconscious desires and aversions, to our natural social instincts. Absorbing, informative, and always intriguing, each book is written by an expert in the field, examining how research-based knowledge compares with popular wisdom, and showing how psychology can truly enrich our understanding of modern life.

Applying a psychological lens to an array of topics and contemporary concerns - from sex, to fashion, to conspiracy theories - *The Psychology of Everything* will make you look at everything in a new way.

For more information about this series, please visit: www.routledgetextbooks.com/textbooks/thepsychologyofeverything/

THE PSYCHOLOGY
OF THE EXTREME

ARIE W. KRUGLANSKI
AND
SOPHIA MOSKALENKO

LONDON AND NEW YORK

First published 2025
by Routledge
4 Park Square, Milton Park, Abingdon, Oxon OX14 4RN

and by Routledge
605 Third Avenue, New York, NY 10158

Routledge is an imprint of the Taylor & Francis Group, an informa business

British Library Cataloguing-in-Publication Data
A catalogue record for this book is available from the British Library

Library of Congress Cataloging-in-Publication Data
Names: Kruglanski, Arie W., author. | Moskalenko, Sophia, author.
Title: Psychology of the extreme / Arie W. Kruglanski and Sophia
Moskalenko.
Description: Abingdon, Oxon; New York, NY: Routledge, 2025. |
Series: The psychology of everything | Includes bibliographical references
and index.
Identifiers: LCCN 2024040626 (print) | LCCN 2024040627 (ebook) |
ISBN 9781032751191 (hardback) | ISBN 9781032751184 (paperback) |
ISBN 9781003472476 (ebook)
Subjects: LCSH: Extreme behavior (Psychology)
Classification: LCC BF637.E97 K78 2025 (print) | LCC BF637.E97 (ebook) |
DDC 155.2/32–dc23/eng/20241025
LC record available at https://lccn.loc.gov/2024040626
LC ebook record available at https://lccn.loc.gov/2024040627

ISBN: 9781032751191 (hbk)
ISBN: 9781032751184 (pbk)
ISBN: 9781003472476 (ebk)

DOI: 10.4324/9781003472476

Typeset in Joanna
by Deanta Global Publishing Services, Chennai, India

CONTENTS

ACKNOWLEDGMENTS

We are grateful to Dr Andreas Beelman, whose invitation to a 2022 workshop on Aggression in Jena, Germany, inspired our collaboration. We are also grateful to Dr Ewa Szumowska, whose research on the psychology of extremism laid the groundwork for the book. Thanks are also due to colleagues and collaborators whose research illustrated and substantiated our chapters, and whose friendship sustains and inspires us: Dr Mia Bloom, Dr Catalina Kopez, and Dr Clark McCauley.

1

EXTREMIST DYNAMICS

What do Van Gogh, Mother Teresa, a foreign terrorist fighter, and the guy next door who spends 12 hours a day playing videogames have in common?

Despite their obvious differences, each of these individuals exhibits a single-track mind, pursuing a single motivation with supreme dedication and to the exclusion of other concerns. Exceptional humanitarianism, fanatic religiosity, indiscriminate political violence that takes no prisoners, and a devouring addiction to a hobby have one thing in common—their extremism. The psychology of extremism, the topic of this book, is that of prioritizing one concern, idée fixe or goal over all others, sometimes with the spectacular results of Van Gogh's breathtaking art or the inspiring compassion of Mother Theresa; other times with the horrific destruction wrought by deadly terrorism, and at yet other times with the effects, whether good or ill, limited to one's personal life and the circle of one's loved ones, such as the effects of extreme videogaming, workaholism, or engagement in extreme sports, on one's own and one's intimates' wellbeing.

This idea of extremism—as a general human tendency that transcends domains and can manifest as both benevolent and evil, magnificent and mundane—may seem uncomfortable and controversial. After all, in the years since 9/11 terrorist attacks, news and political discourse have been using the term "violent extremism" over and over—to describe acts of political violence and opinions that

DOI: 10.4324/9781003472476-1

justify it. We have been trained by the media to hear "extremism" and think "violent extremism." The broad perspective on extremism that we are presenting may thus seem counter-intuitive, in light of our media-induced habit of equating "extremism" with mayhem and destruction. But the tradeoff for overcoming this mental bias is a deeper understanding of a phenomenon that is not rare or distant but widespread and likely familiar to some readers as either their own or a loved one's tendency. Indeed, as we show later, the phenomenon of extremism is mere exaggeration of something very adaptive and necessary for survival: our ability to focus at times of emergency on a single objective, while momentarily "forgetting" all else. Even when extremism transcends situations of emergency and becomes part of one's lifestyle, it isn't necessarily bad. Like with most things in life, it is a matter of tradeoffs: great upheavals and drama versus peaceful routine. The real problem arises when extremism's consequences turn pernicious and toxic, both to the extremists themselves and to others impacted by their actions.

The limited and frightening view that equates extremism with violence leaves much of its psychology obscured, and with it leaves out the possibility of better understanding it. Most importantly, it contains no helpful clues for detecting extremism early, as well as for mitigating, countering, or redirecting it into constructive rather than destructive directions. Based on our general depiction of extremism's psychological dynamics, we describe in this book empirically grounded approaches and interventions which may be fruitful in either reducing extremist tendencies or redirecting them. We hope to leave the reader more alert and better equipped: alert to extremism's immense psychological power for good or ill, and equipped to recognize and effectively handle external and internal inducements to extremism.

WHY READ A BOOK ON EXTREMISM NOW?

Doesn't it seem like everything used to be just a little easier?

Getting a well-paying job, getting into college, finding love, making friends, feeling good about yourself, it all seemed to have been less of a struggle generations ago. But life has become so much faster, so much more demanding. Unrelenting pressure is the new normal.

Nobody works a nine-to-five job anymore, answering professional emails and texting day and night—and that's if they can even get a paid job after college. College admission, which used to depend on good grades from high school, now favors candidates who score above everyone on everything and have had a few publications or a successful startup by age 18. Instagram fashion trends are driving up the rates of depression and self-harm among teenage girls;[1] they used to have their hands full just with fitting in with their friends at school—but now they compete with millions of Instagram users photoshopped and filtered into enviable paragons of beauty and sex appeal. Primary school kids, who a couple of generations ago spent their leisure time climbing trees in the backyard, are now pushed to enroll into multiple competitive activities, as their parents strive to measure up to the impossible standards of both parenthood and childhood achievement.[2] Going to the gym used to be good enough for keeping in shape, but now the shape to strive for is not attainable without the benefits—and costs—of steroids.[3] Plastic surgery to keep younger; ever more possessions to keep up with the Joneses; ever higher achievements to keep up with the standards rising to the stars (who are "just like us," haven't you heard?).

THE AGE OF EXTREMISM

The times we live in may well be called *the Age of Extremism*. Extremist politics tear our society asunder, violent extremists threaten our stability and security, extreme consumption of billionaires like Musk and Bezos set new standards of self-indulgence, and extreme authoritarians like Trump, Bolsonaro, Putin, or Netanyahu are turning the world order upside-down. Whether we are aware of it or not, the mounting political, economic, and social pressures nudge us all to extremism in countless ways. And in this world of informational deluge delivered by social media we strain to extreme to have our voice heard above the rising din of the general chatter.

The French political philosopher Montesquieu (1748) once stated that "mankind are governed not by extremes, but by principles of moderation." That may have been then, but this is now. What used to be extreme became mainstream. And there is a price to pay.

This book is about extremism in people's personal lives, and in the larger society. As psychologists, we have researched a particular kind of extremism that is socially destructive, the hateful and violent kind—radicalization that progresses to terrorism. Yet even in terrorism, we see changes reflecting a faster, more interconnected life. Less Al Qaeda-type terrorist groups in faraway mountains; more ISIS-type radicals that recruit online from around the world, more right-wing militia groups next door.

But destructive extremism is not necessarily confined to the evening news. People can be personally extreme, destroying their bodies through unmoderated exercise, diet, or drugs; developing extreme thought patterns that turn into depression, anxiety, or social isolation; or cultivating extreme habits of substance abuse. In the USA, personal extremism has been on the rise, with both loneliness[4] and mental illness[5] surging in the last few years, as has the number of individuals involved in terrorism-related crimes.[6]

But there is good news as well. As noted earlier, extremism is not always damaging or destructive. In fact, positive social change has often been achieved through extremism. Great science, great art, and social justice sometimes were the fruits of utter dedication and self-sacrifice born of individuals' propensity to extremism. Thanks to Maria Sklodowska-Curie's extreme dedication to science, we have the benefits of her discoveries in chemistry and medicine; because of Martin Luther King's extreme opposition to the oppression of Blacks in the USA, the oppressive laws were overhauled; India owes its independence from the British Empire to Gandhi's extreme devotion this cause. Scientific, political and historical changes achieved through these and other cases of constructive extremism have made the world a better place.

And there are positive kinds of personal extremism. Falling in love can be an extreme experience, but one that can lead to personal growth, elevation, and lifelong companionship. Likewise, extreme dedication to a career, a hobby or to art can lead to self-development, learning, and social connectedness.

It is intriguing how the same psychology that explains the destructive varieties of extremism underlies also the pro-social, constructive kinds. Going beyond the established norms, breaking rules and boundaries, challenging conventions and singularly pursuing an idea or an objective are not exclusive to terrorists and political radicals but often drives progress in all areas of life. That their core psychology is similar hardly implies a moral equivalence between destructive and constructive extremisms. The two are diametric opposites in the desirability of their outcomes and consequences. Like nuclear power, this elemental potential of going to the extreme can warm and illuminate, but it can also kill and annihilate. Yet understanding the common denominator of diverse extremisms is the first step in being able to manage them. Our purpose in this book is to offer such an understanding and address the questions how does one decide between extremism and moderation, and how does one redirect destructive into constructive extremism. We thus cast our net widely to identify the essential psychology beyond the bewildering diversity of extremisms, and share with our readers research-based insights into how to survive and thrive in this age of extremism.

Extremism is upon us, it is here to stay, and it calls for new adjustments. These require getting to know it, recognizing its pitfalls, and appreciating the possibilities it offers.

EXTREMISM AND TEA

A Buddhist parable speaks of a great demon, Mara, who kept tempting and testing the Buddha with greed, anger, lust, doubt. And although Buddha fought Mara off every time, he could not prevail: Mara came back in different disguises and challenged the Buddha again and again. Until one day, instead of fighting Mara, Buddha said, "I see you, Mara," and invited the demon to tea. From then on, Mara would show up from time to time, but instead of a struggle, Buddha would say, "I see you, Mara," and invite the demon to tea, and they would sit together, and then part peacefully.

The "inviting to tea" approach can have profound effects in the real world of the 21st century as well, it seems. Don Ritchie, an Australian who lived near a cliff in Sydney called The Gap—a location known for multiple suicide attempts, rescued at least 180 people from jumping to their deaths. Noticing someone at the cliff in apparent distress, Ritchie would strike a conversation with them and invite them back to his home for a cup of tea and a chat. Some of the people he helped would return years later to thank him.

Extremism, like demon Mara, comes in many forms. Sometimes, it presents as suicidal depression that drives a person to The Gap; other times, extremism manifests as greed, or as reckless risk-taking. The Buddhist story and Don Ritchie's remarkable success both suggest a counter-intuitive remedy for extremism-driven destruction: to acknowledge the extreme, to face it, and, by taking time with it, to disarm it, ushering in moderation. This book offers the readers a chance to do just that: to spend time with extremism, to recognize it under the many disguises it wears—including within ourselves—and to learn how to redirect or diffuse its dangers.

But the story of sitting down for tea with extremism is about more than just taming one's demons or guarding against demons outside the door. The Buddha gained enlightenment when he chose to serve Mara tea. Don Ritchie's dedication to offering tea to would-be jumpers imbued his life with meaning, and gifted life to those who were about to throw it away. Understanding extremism in ourselves and others extends the promise of such enlightenment.

ON A PERSONAL NOTE: WE THE EXTREMISTS

As we invite the reader to explore the many faces of extremism, we feel compelled to make a confession. You see, under our definition, we ourselves are extremists of sorts. It so happens that each of us was so preoccupied with one goal that we dedicated most of our time to it, risking our own safety in the pursuit.

Arie. Arie's extremism story (one of them…) illustrates a case of extremism in an extreme situation, namely during the October 1973 (Yom Kippur) war when the forces of Egypt and Syria launched a deadly surprise attack on Israel. An Israeli army reservist at the time, Arie was called to duty. His special mission as an Israeli Defense Forces (IDF) psychology officer was to scout the two major fronts, in the Sinai desert bordering Egypt and the Golan Heights bordering Syria, trying to understand the fighters' state of mind and ways in which it could be boosted. With the bullets and the artillery shells flying, it wasn't an easy job. But for an extremist, things like wars and imminent risk of being killed or maimed are only distractions from their main focus. Arie had a burning problem that—to him— was crucial: a deadline for an academic psychology paper! And so, being an extremist where it came to his academic pursuits, Arie kept working on the paper amidst the surrounding chaos, uproar, and the awfulness of war, totally shutting out the drama, the tension, and the raging struggle around him. While everyone else on the team was taking shelter and resting after a harrowing day of field work with the troops, Arie was making edits to his paper using a flashlight for illumination, and with deafening artillery blasts in the background. The war fortunately ended with IDF repelling the attack. And on an infinitely lesser note, Arie's paper met the deadline, vindicating his capacity for extremism… this time around.

Arie's story paints a striking picture of just how far extremists can go in neglecting the world around them when they are pursuing their passions. Not even flying bullets are enough to take their eyes off the goal. It also shows the trademark insensitivity to "what's normal" shared by all extremists. In life-or-death situations, most people mobilize all their resources to survive, and to hell with things like academic papers and deadlines. But for extremists, the broader field of reality outside of their singular focus is blurry, and unlike most people they overlook or purposefully ignore it, the better to direct their resources to the one thing they care most about.

Sophia. As a high school student in Ukraine, Sophia dreamed of becoming a psychologist. There was only one problem: not a single college or university in the country had a psychology department. The former USSR just collapsed, but its legacy persisted, including communist ideas that an individual was not a legitimate unit of consideration, that only the collective mattered, reflected in the academic and professional offerings available at the time. But these limits would not deter Sophia. With no money and very little English, she got into a student exchange program to visit the USA, the best country to study psychology, hoping to somehow become a student there. As you might imagine, it was considerably more complicated than she could have imagined from the little she knew about the USA, her knowledge derived primarily from bootlegged Hollywood movies she had watched back home. The reality was far more brutal.

At one point Sophia found herself unhoused, undocumented, working 14-hour days as a waitress in a diner, and without much hope of advancing beyond this dead-end. Facing a choice between giving up a dream of becoming a psychologist and going back home or persevering in a strange country despite overwhelming odds, many people would have given up. But being a kind of extremist, Sophia was fixated on her goal, rather unreasonably. Luckily, after much tragedy and tribulation, she succeeded, winning a full scholarship to the college of her dreams, graduated Magna Cum Laude with Special distinction in Psychology, and proceeded to go to a PhD psychology program in an Ivy League university.

Sophia's story exemplifies another side of extremism: sometimes it can move mountains, overcome overwhelming obstacles, and reach impossible dreams. But even in stories with a happy ending, such as Sophia's, extremism exerts a toll.

THIS BOOK

Our book thus aims to offer the broader psychological perspective on extremism. In doing so, we will identify outside forces that can foster extremism, as well as internal, personality qualities that make one likely to be extreme about even ordinary, day-to-day pursuits. Knowing these "risk factors" will offer a possibility of addressing them, giving readers some control over their own extremist tendencies—if any. We describe different kinds of extremism, some constructive and beneficial, others destructive and harmful. Understanding that extremism can be either pro-social or anti-social in its aims implies that people "on the dark side" can "turn to the light," using their extreme dedication for good rather than evil—our case studies will demonstrate this transformation (see Chapters 4, 6, and 10).

IN SUMMARY

Extremism is rooted in the human potential for motivational imbalance, and the ability to prioritize a single issue or concern to the exclusion of all else. Such single-mindedness could focus on any issue whatsoever, so unlike the common use, where the term "extremism" denotes terrorism and political violence, the same psychological dynamic that accounts for these accounts also for all other types of extremism (extreme sports, extreme diets, extreme romantic crushes, exceptional humanism). It also follows from this analysis that some extremisms can have positive social consequences, whereas others—highly negative ones. Common to both, however, are the costs incurred by the extremists themselves. By forgetting all else, apart from their focal concern, the extremists leave some of their basic needs unmet, which typically exerts a toll on their physical and mental health and their wellbeing. To sum up then, we aim here to introduce you, dear reader, to something that should need no introduction, perhaps, as it exists around us all in its myriad manifestations. But the secret psychology of extremism that lurks beyond its surface expressions is less widely known or immediately apparent. It is this psychology that we aim to describe in the pages that follow.

NOTES

1 Choukas-Bradley, S., Roberts, S. R., Maheux, A. J., & Nesi, J. (2022). The perfect storm: A developmental–sociocultural framework for the role of social media in adolescent girls' body image concerns and mental health. *Clinical Child and Family Psychology Review, 25*(4), 681–701.

2 Snellman, K., Silva, J. M., Frederick, C. B., & Putnam, R. D. (2015). The engagement gap: Social mobility and extracurricular participation among American youth. *The ANNALS of the American Academy of Political and Social Science, 657*(1), 194–207. https://doi.org/10.1177/0002716214548398

3 Ricciardelli, L. A., McCabe, M. P., Lillis, J., & Thomas, K. (2006). A longitudinal investigation of the development of weight and muscle concerns among preadolescent boys. *Journal of Youth and Adolescence, 35*(2), 168–178. https://doi.org/10.1007/s10964-005-9004-7

4 Corbin, I. M., & Waters, J. (2023, May 16). What the surgeon general missed about America's loneliness epidemic. *Capita.* https://www.capita.org/capita-ideas/2023/05/16/what-the-surgeon-general-missed-about-americas-loneliness-epidemic1

5 Warren, D. (2021, November 1). The state of mental health in America 2022: Adult prevalence and access to care. *NextStep Solutions* (blog). https://www.nssbehavioralhealth.com/nss-blog-the-state-of-mental-health-in-america-2022-adult-prevalence-and-access-to-care/

6 U.S. Government Accountability Office. (2023, March 2). The rising threat of domestic terrorism in the U.S. and federal efforts to combat it. *U.S. GAO.* https://www.gao.gov/blog/rising-threat-domestic-terrorism-u.s.-and-federal-efforts-combat-it

2

GOOD EXTREMISM, BAD EXTREMISM

Extremism is a state of psychological imbalance, a "one-track-mindedness" where a person's exaggerated focus on one concern overshadows all others. For an extremist, any means are justified in service of their singular pursuit. Such is the case with addictions—whether to substances like drugs or alcohol or to behavior patterns like video gaming, or hoarding, or indeed to one's career—spawning workaholism that leads people to neglect other aspects of their lives.

A TALE OF TWO EXTREMISTS

Imagine a young man from an affluent Asian family. Growing up, he is an average student, rather shy with peers, not a leader among friends. But in his teenage years, the young man becomes deeply engaged with philosophical and religious ideas. He starts to eat, dress, and act differently than his friends, becoming an odd one out among them. He demands that his family members follow him in shunning worldly indulgences to instead pursue the path to moral clarity and self-sacrifice he chose for himself. He studies at the university, marries young, as customary in his community, and joins the family trade. But instead of the usual ambitions of young professionals, the young man uses his profession to promote the ideological cause he is

DOI: 10.4324/9781003472476-2

increasingly invested in. Gradually, his social circle narrows to those who agree with his ideological commitment, whereas those who doubt or disagree fall by the wayside. A greater focus on the cause calls for greater sacrifices, and the young man risks his safety, his freedom, and even his life to advance the ideals he is so invested in.

His extraordinary actions draw attention of the press. The publicity brings him fame with some people and infamy with others. In his extremism, he becomes an inspiration to millions around the world, as well as anathema of hatred and fear for millions of others. His name becomes synonymous with his cause. His many detractors carry out repeated attempts on his life and eventually manage to assassinate him.

Can you guess the name of this man?

This is a trick question. We wrote the extremist profile so that not one but two men would fit it. We are all but certain that you have heard of both.

One is Mohandas Gandhi, known around the world as Mahatma (Great Soul) Gandhi.[1] Born into a well-to-do family—his father was the chief minister of the province—young Gandhi was shy and introverted, and by his own admission he wasn't a particularly gifted student. He entered into an arranged marriage at the age of 13, and at 18 he traveled to London to study law, following in the footsteps of his older brother. However, in London Gandhi found himself troubled. He detested Western food, Western dress, and Western traditions (such as ballroom dancing) and questioned Western moral values. Upon graduation, Gandhi returned to India briefly before traveling to South Africa. It was there that his opposition to Western colonialism and institutionalized mistreatment of "coloreds" crystalized into *satyagraha*, a policy of passive resistance that Gandhi formulated from deep reflection on the Bhagavad Gita, the New Testament, and the work of philosophers like Henry Thoreau and Leo Tolstoy. Gandhi used his law degree and his rhetorical skills to write and speak publicly about his beliefs, gaining admiration from some and contempt from others, leading protests that often resulted in his physical injury and imprisonment, staging hunger strikes, and suffering repeated attempts on his life.

Gandhi's resistance to Western values included resistance to Western temptations, such as indulgences in food, comforts, and luxury. Having himself given up Western clothes for a loincloth and shawl that he hand-made, and limiting his diet to only raw fruits and nuts, Gandhi demanded that his wife give up her heirloom jewelry and that their children be refused Western medicine for their ailments. It is believed that Gandhi's wife, Kasturbai, would not have succumbed to malaria if she had taken quinine, the Western medical treatment that Gandhi opposed. Gandhi's extremism—his steadfast dedication to the idea of resistance to Western values, his personal example and self-sacrifice—was crucial to India's success in achieving independence from the British Empire, inspiring the peaceful resistance movements led by Martin Luther King in the USA and Nelson Mandela in South Africa.

Gandhi is a celebrated example of *constructive extremism*: extreme dedication whose effects benefit society by advancing it culturally, morally, technologically, or scientifically. Innovation often depends on extremists to overcome resistance to traditional norms and entrenched power structures. Voltaire said, "Our wretched species is so made that those who walk on the well-trodden path always throw stones at those who are showing a new road." More temperate characters might waver from a new path, compromising on their ideas and values, going along to get along. But extremists take the road less traveled and charge forward no matter the costs. We reap the benefits of constructive extremists' relentless pursuit of innovative ideas every day: when we partake of the freedoms hard-won in revolutions and protest movements, when we enjoy the products of scientific knowledge for which early trailblazers were tortured by the Inquisition, or when we use technology such as computers or airplanes, whose proliferation was advanced by extremists ridiculed for their vision.

Interestingly, the anonymous profile of extremism depicted above fits another case, that of *destructive extremism*. That is the case of the world's most notorious terrorist, Osama bin Laden.

A shy and gangly son of a Saudi construction tycoon, Osama bin Laden was not a particularly stellar student at school. He wasn't known for his leadership skills in his youth. Contemporaries recall him as a courteous and polite teenager, not prone to anger or violence.

In his late teens, bin Laden began developing an extreme devotion to religious ideas. At about age 14, he joined an Islamic study group inspired by the ideas of Muslim Brotherhood, proclaiming that only a government according to the Koran—Sharia government—could offer Muslim countries freedom from the oppression and colonial rule of the West. Bin Laden's dedication to these ideas grew, and with it grew the magnitude of his sacrifices: following Islamic laws, he stopped watching television except for news, stopped wearing shorts and short-sleeved shirts, stopped playing cards, participating in teenage banter about girls—in fact, he stopped looking at women's faces unless they were his sisters or mother. He began fasting two days per week as the Prophet did. At one point, bin Laden demanded that his mother and stepfamily stop watching television. A friend recalled that bin Laden expressed pronounced moral opprobrium when his youth soccer teammates wore shorts rather than the long pants prescribed under Islamic law.

At 17, Osama married, and two years later began his studies at King Abdul University in Jeddah. Although he was supposed to focus on economics and management, he was more interested in religious activities. After completing his studies, bin Laden got a job at his father's construction company, but his career took a sharply different turn when the Soviets invaded Afghanistan in 1979, bringing with them the kind of godless colonialism bin Laden was so opposed to. He directed his management skills and his company resources to first sponsoring Afghan resistance, then joining it, using his construction equipment to dig trenches and fortification, and then founding training camps for jihadi fighters from around the world. While driving a bulldozer under Soviet fire in Eastern Afghanistan's Khowost, bin Laden was wounded. Undeterred, he and his men withstood Soviet attacks, gaining him fame as a hero among the mujahedeen—fame which only grew when the Soviets withdrew from Afghanistan in 1988.

Bin Laden rode the wave of that political momentum to broaden the fight from Afghanistan to fighting infidels in other Muslim lands, and co-founded Al Qaeda with several like-minded fundamentalist Islamists. He began to speak out against US presence in Saudi Arabia, rousing the ire of both the USA and the Saudi government, which resulted in his arrest and the revocation of his passport. This marked the beginning of bin Laden's fight against what he saw as apostate Muslim governments, Western colonialism, and moral corruption that the West inflicted on Muslims around the world. As an extremist, bin Laden dedicated his resources, spent his own and his family's money, risked his wellbeing, his freedom and his life, and finally ended up being killed by a US special forces raid for his role as the mastermind of the deadliest terrorist attack against the USA in history on September 11, 2001.

Clearly, bin Laden's extremism was destructive. The terror attacks of 9/11 that bin Laden sponsored and directed killed thousands of innocent people. What's more, the 9/11 attacks were planned by bin Laden and his right-hand man, Ayman al-Zawahiri, as a jujitsu move, and they succeeded as such, triggering a massive over-reaction by the US government that resulted in two wars in the Middle East with casualties numbering in hundreds of thousands and ripple effects still reverberating decades later in deadly political violence around the world.

Although it may seem jarring to even mention the saintly Mahatma Gandhi in the same breath as the murderous bin Laden, the psychological similarities between their two cases are striking. Both men came from privileged backgrounds. Both were shy and unremarkable in their youth. Both came of age in an Asian country subjected to Western colonial culture. Both opposed this influence and dedicated their lives to fighting it. Their sacrifices for the cause began early and grew with time: first changing how they dressed, what they ate, with whom they associated; then trying to convert their families to their cause; then dedicating their careers, risking their safety, freedom, and lives for it. Both became world famous (or notorious) for their extremism. Ultimately both died for their cause.

Anguish. Constructive or destructive, extremism affects the extremists themselves as well as other people. For extremists, over-focusing on the dominant object of their attention leads to neglecting essential personal concerns: a drug addict, a gambler, or an inveterate video gamer pays a high personal price for their indulgence. A work-aholic, a "mad scientist" overfocused on their research, and a "starv-ing artist" pursuing their inspiration no matter what their critics or their bank accounts say suffer the consequences of their extremism in diminished wellbeing and social isolation. Families and friends of extremists have to either follow them on their deviant path or be gone from their world.

Indeed, separation from mainstream family and friends is a con-sistent correlate of extremism. This was so for Osama bin Laden whose religious devotion estranged him from family and friends. It was so for Mahatma Gandhi, who came to despise the Western norms and lifestyles embraced by members of his social circle. It is so for the extremists "next door" who may never gain the world fame of Gandhi or notoriety of bin Laden, but whose intense pas-sions create a similar break with their less adamant intimates. The isolation of Gandhi and bin Laden ended when by their charisma and conviction they managed to convince others to follow in their footsteps—thus creating a new social network with its own unique norms. Less capable influencers, however, may remain in isolation unless they find similarly-minded others.

Extremist's progress. An extremist's deviation could begin innoc-uously enough, as an unusual preference or interest to which hardly anyone in the individual's circle attaches much significance. Suppose a teenager suddenly develops an insatiable appetite for some activity, be it bodybuilding or building model trains. While initially tolerated, if not encouraged, by the parents, the new hobby begins to assume gargantuan proportions. It consumes more and more of the indi-vidual's waking hours, and their schooling and chores are increas-ingly sacrificed on the altar of the overriding new passion. Maybe they get in trouble for it: spend their parents' money on their hobby, skip school, and sneak out of the house after curfew in pursuit of their obsession. Maybe they flaunt the social norms they see as irrelevant, or as distracting: maybe they begin to dress funny and act weird. They don't have time or interest to pursue activities popular among their friends, and so in social interactions they often seem "out of touch," visibly withdrawn and isolated rather than participating in lively discussions. How would parents, teachers, and peers react to their swerving so off the beaten path? Typically, with anxiety and concern.

The parents might try to persuade, cajole, or bribe their child to re-engage in chores and family functions, to spend more time on schoolwork and friends and less time on their obsession. The teachers might seek to re-engage the student in academic tasks and social functions. The peers might crack jokes about the "weirdo," sneer at and mock their unusual behavior; the kinder ones might try to bring the would-be extremist back into the social fold by showing them affection and acceptance. Their pleas might in some cases resonate with the budding extremist and succeed in bringing them back into the fold. Indeed, the social circle—family, caring adults or peers—is the first line of defense against extremism. It responds to the obvious evidence of someone's veering off from the straight and narrow by trying to pull them back into their midst by a variety of means.

GROUP INFLUENCE

The power and influence of the group over its members is well known to social scientists. Even artificial groups that psychologists cobble together out of perfect strangers in their experimental laboratories, "quasi-groups" that only exist for the brief duration of an experimental study, almost immediately begin to function as strong social norm drivers. Within minutes of sitting in the same room with some strangers, we look to them for clues about how to behave, what to say, to what attend. In one famous study, participants were asked to report out loud when the experimenter asked them which of the three lines on a card was the same length as a comparison line. When participants were alone with the experimenter, they called out the correct line every time—they had no trouble seeing the right answer. But when they were placed in a group of the experimenter's associates who pretended to be "other participants" and who unanimously called out the wrong line, by the time it was the real participant's turn to answer, one out of three people said exactly what the group said, following the norm rather than the evidence of their eyes.

In another experiment, participants were asked to fill out some questionnaires in a waiting room with other participants who were actually, as in the study above, associates of the experimenter. A little while later, the waiting room began filling with thick white smoke. What would anyone do in this situation? Leave the room, call security, or call 911, right? Wrong. The answer, the experiment demonstrated, depended on what other people in the room were doing: when "other participants" continued to fill out their questionnaires nonchalantly, as though the smoke did not exist, the real participants remained seated in a smoke-filling room even when the smoke got so thick that they had to bring the questionnaires closer to their faces to see what was on them. In other words, even in emergency situations that threaten wellbeing or life, we are likely to follow group norms—and even though the groups in these studies were "ad-hoc"—created in the spur of the moment with nothing in common. Just imagine how much stronger social norms can be in a real-life group, where people share a common history, interpersonal attachments, and a common future.

It may seem silly or unreasonable that people would betray the evidence of their own eyes and jeopardize their own safety to follow social norms, but there are deep-rooted evolutionary reasons to maintain harmony within social units to maximize their survival.[2] Over the millennia of human existence, groups that could maintain strong social norms were more likely to persist, maintaining strong interpersonal and inter-generational connections, whereas those where social norms were weak were more likely to disperse and perish, taking down with them their social-norms-flaunting genes. Facing challenges of primordial life, including hunting and gathering, protecting from elements and predators, and competing with rival groups, strong social norms allowed our ancestors to coordinate group efforts, which increased their chances for survival. As a result of these evolutionary pressures, social norms are an inescapable companion of human interactions, from early childhood to late adulthood, from Amazonian tribes to megapolis dwellers, from small groups to ethnicities and nations. Cross-culturally, violators of social norms face punishment or ostracism[3] from others, even if those others are mere observers and are not personally affected by the norm violation. This "altruistic punishment" tendency is believed to have evolved alongside human sociality to protect the integrity of groups by protecting social norms. These sanctions leave norm violators with two options: they can either adjust their behavior to better fit the norm, or they can face further distancing from the group and endure the anxiety this induces.

Extremists become norm violators by overfocusing on their singular interests to the exclusion of other domains deemed important by others around them. Teenagers in our society are expected to go to school, socialize, and maintain some extracurricular interests; they are not supposed to drop everything in favor of a single obsession. The pressure exerted by those who witness an individual's budding extremism, whether this pressure is expressed as kind concern, as ridicule, as appeals to reason and duty, or as ostracism, can work to reduce extremism and bring the individual back into the normative fold.

In the case of our would-be teenage extremist, the combined efforts of parents, teachers, and peers to tone down their obsession can have the same two outcomes. Either the kid limits the amount of time and effort spent on the cause they've been preoccupied with, or they persevere in their extremism and widen the chasm between themselves and people in their lives, becoming socially isolated, and hence removing the constraints to spending inordinate time and resources on the object of their passion, in a kind of self-reinforcing cycle.

Helping such a cycle develop in this era of social media is the easy availability of connecting with similarly-minded others who share one's obsession and so provide social support (and reinforcement) for one's extremism. Literally at one's fingertips, social media allows connecting with other extremists online, no matter how esoteric and deviant from the mainstream their interests happen to be.

Finding or forming a group that shares and supports one's extremism is typically crucial to maintaining it. The vast majority of people need to be accepted and respected. To be lonely in one's deviance is difficult to bear, and likely to draw the extremist back to the mainstream.

Indeed, extreme behaviors are not very common. Many different types of extremisms attest to this. For instance, internet addiction has been found in around 2% of studied samples.[4] The prevalence of video game addiction is found in 0.6%–2% of the samples.[5] The prevalence of exercise addiction[6] is around 2.5%–3%.[7] Black and Carver (2007) report that the lifetime prevalence of addictive shopping is about 5.8%. Slightly above 4% of the samples studied showed symptoms of Internet sex addiction of magnitude sufficient for interference with major areas of life.[8]

Extreme dieting is also rare and occurs primarily among older adolescents or young adults (mostly women).[9] Among dieting adolescents only 1%–8.9% reported using potentially dangerous weight loss methods. Exaggerated dieting decreases with age[10] and only a few sustain it for long, with 0.4% reaching its clinical form (i.e. anorexia nervosa).[11]

IT'S LONELY AT THE EDGE

Social isolation does not necessarily follow extremism—sometimes it can precede it. A person can be bullied or ostracized by peers because they are unusually smart, or unusually tall, or because of the kind of family they come from, their ethnicity or religion, or some other quality that has nothing to do with extremism. Being socially isolated means that the time that others spend socializing is available to the individual to pursue some interest. And without social norms from a peer group to rein in an interest, it can turn into an obsession that takes over every waking hour, every thought, and every intention.

For Gandhi, isolation was the consequence of going to London to study law. Not only was he alone in a strange country, without family or friends, but he was feeling especially isolated because of his status as an ethnic and religious minority. What's more, because he was a vegetarian, the typical social occasion of taking meals became instead a source of frustration and further isolation. Perhaps this disconnection from a social network in London was what initiated Gandhi's extreme interests in philosophy and in anti-Western, anti-colonial ideas. When he arrived in South Africa, Gandhi experienced an event that his autobiography describes as pivotal in his evolution from thinker to activist. Because he was Indian, Gandhi was ordered to move to the third-class train car, even though he held a first-class ticket. When he refused, Gandhi was thrown out of the train. Spending a cold night alone on a train platform, Gandhi decided to pursue the extremist path that defined his life and made him world-famous. That traumatic sense of social rejection and isolation, perhaps felt especially keenly after his unfortunate London experiences, likely spurred Gandhi onto an extreme course of action that made history.

For Osama bin Laden, the isolation seemed largely self-induced. His early distaste for all forms of Western entertainment so appealing to his peers (television, Westerns, colorful magazines with images of women), and his concomitant rejection of individuals who failed to follow his ascetic example marked his growing separation from his erstwhile friends. Luckily for him, he found a group of others who shared his views, members of the Islamic Study group. The social norms that would have limited his extremism—those of his high school friends and soccer teammates—no longer contained bin Laden. And his newly chosen group only exacerbated his extremism.

Famous cases of extremists, constructive or destructive, often feature a history of social isolation. Steve Jobs, the founder of Apple Computers and Pixar, the mastermind of iPhone, iPad, and other ingenious devices has redefined electronic communications. His design genius benefited greatly from his extreme engagement with the ideas that at the time were nothing short of revolutionary. The history of Jobs' extremism can be traced to his childhood, where his unusually high intellectual abilities made him stand out from his peers, skip over grades in primary school, and seek intellectual challenges beyond what school could offer. With such unusual intelligence, it is not surprising, perhaps, that Jobs was not very socially connected growing up. The label "loner" accompanied him from grade school through middle school (where he was bullied) through high school where he was described by a classmate as "kind of brain and kind of hippie" without ever fitting fit into either group. Smart enough to be a nerd, he, nonetheless, wasn't nerdy. And he was too intellectual for the hippies, "who just wanted to get wasted all the time." This made him an outsider."[12]

Not really fitting in, Jobs spent nearly all his time pursuing his interest in electric engineering. At 13, Steve Jobs cold-called Bill Hewlett (of Hewlett Packard) to ask him for parts for an electronic project he was working on.[13] Although it is unusual and inappropriate for a teenager to bother that way a president of a major company, Jobs got lucky. The nearly unimaginable happened and the phone call got him a summer job at the computer giant. In high school, Jobs befriended Steve Wozniak, and by Jobs' senior year they were selling electronic devices of their own design. Notably, the devices were illegal: their function was to manipulate telephone networks into allowing long-distance phone calls for free. Being an extremist, however, Jobs' concern for rules, norms, and regulations was minimal.

This was also reflected in how Jobs dressed. A neighbor on Crist Drive recalled Jobs greeting clients "with his underwear hanging out, barefoot and hippie-like." As a CEO of Apple, Jobs raved about an idea of a uniform for employees[14] that they adamantly rejected.

So Jobs instituted a uniform just for himself, a now iconic $175.00[15] combination of a black turtleneck and blue jeans that the multimillionaire wore every day.

Jobs was apparently not very keen on common norms of personal hygiene, to the point that some colleagues at Atari, his early employer, refused to work with him. Later, when as a CEO of Apple, the team would force Jobs to take showers before they let him into meetings[16] (p. 82).

And as with our other examples of extremism, Jobs developed very unusual eating habits, fasting for two days at a time, or eating only carrots, which colored his skin into a yellowish tinge.[17] He limited his food to the extreme, excluding all meats, gluten, and high cholesterol foods, and at times eating very little and only vegan or fruitarian foods.

In a commencement address he delivered to Stanford graduating class of 2005, Jobs summarized his recipe for success, which also reflected his views of social norms.

> Your time is limited, so don't waste it living someone else's life. Don't be trapped by dogma—which is living with the results of other people's thinking. Don't let the noise of others' opinions drown out your own inner voice. And most important, have the courage to follow your heart and intuition. They somehow already know what you truly want to become. Everything else is secondary.[18]

Some interesting commonalities emerge from the brief summaries of the three extreme individuals: Osama bin Laden, Mohandas Gandhi, and Steve Jobs.

THE EXTREME PERSONALITY

First, it seems as though in each case, some "foreshadowing" of future extremism could already be glimpsed in the person's childhood. Is it true, one might wonder, that a future extremist can be identified early on by looking at their behaviors and social interactions? The short answer is that we don't know—yet. Ewa Szumowska and colleagues are researching the intriguing possibility that there is something like an "extremist personality" which might run in families and which might be evident early on. Their findings and ways of measuring your own extremism are discussed in Chapter 3.

According to some testimonies, extremism seems to show its signs early on; but it is also possible that once a person becomes famous as an extremist, others' recollections of them tend to focus on the "early signs" that might have been otherwise forgotten or interpreted differently, painting a picture of the past colored by knowledge of the present.

We all have done something extreme, and teenage years is when most of us flirt with norm violation. Usually, these instances are forgotten. But if any one of us were one day to wake up and decide to pursue an idea to the extreme, and end up world-famous for that pursuit, friends and family might find themselves recollecting our youthful indiscretions as they try to wrap their minds around our evolution. In other words, the early history of extremism may be a case of biased recall rather than diagnostic developmental feature.

Second, it's interesting that all three individuals we described in this chapter became extreme about their eating habits. Gandhi maintained his vegetarianism in meat-eating London, and then became a fruitarian, eating only raw fruits and nuts. Bin Laden began fasting two days a week as a teenager. And Steve Jobs did both: he fasted and severely limited the foods he ate, with the rationale that limiting the energy it takes to digest food means that it can be used for creativity instead.

Indeed, many extremists we have researched for this book have had a quirky diet. Hitler was a moral vegetarian. Nicola Tesla went on extreme fasts. Honore de Balzac drank 50 cups of espresso so he could write through the night (he eventually died of caffeine poisoning!)[19] Charles Darwin explored not just remote islands but also eating unusual species, such as owls, hawks, armadillos and iguanas. In short, there is no shortage of extreme diets among famous extremists.

Extremists' quirky eating habits might stem from their relationship to social norms. Food, after all, is one of the most social pastimes, and it is regulated by a host of norms: what is appropriate to eat (e.g. organ meats are not considered appropriate as food by most Americans, who might gag at blood sausage greatly enjoyed by Ukrainians or at fermented eggs beloved by Chinese); how much food is appropriate to consume (little at a fancy French restaurant; lots at an all you can eat buffet); what is immoral to eat at all (pigs for Muslims and Jews, meat for vegetarians, honey for vegans). For extremists, who have at best a tenuous relationship with social norms, norms that govern food and eating are as inconsequential as any others. Because food is a daily ritual, it takes up time; eating in company takes up even more time—and for an extremist that time seems much better spent doing what they are obsessed about.

A striking example of an utter disregard for eating norms was Isaac Newton, a workaholic, who neglected eating in favor of his extreme pursuit of scientific ideas for 18 or 19 hours a day.

> He would forget to eat and, when reminded that he had left his food untouched, would exclaim, "Have I!" before eating a little while still standing. He never bothered to sit down for his meals. This is the portrait of a man in the grip of an inspiration, or an obsession, that would never let him rest.[20]

The price. Focusing predominantly on one idea, pursuit or activity as extremists do comes at a cost. Sometimes, that cost is limited to the extremist and only the closest circle of their family and closest companions. Extreme diets, extreme lifestyles, social isolation, indifference to basic comforts can exert a high toll, even lead to illness and death as it did for Balzac.

Other times, however, the extremists sacrifice other people's wellbeing and even lives in pursuit of their goals. Destructive extremists like Osama bin Laden see their ideas as far more important than people's lives. For the broader society, extremists' neglect of other people's concerns, viewing them as means to extremists' own ends, or worse yet as enemies who deserve destruction or annihilation, can foster social ills such as crime, corruption, and political conflict. When shared by large groups of people, this kind of extremism can polarize societies, divide people into "us and them," and promote an "insider morality" in which whatever serves one's group is just and right—as was the case with German Nazism in World War II, and is the case with current Russian nationalism that fuels Russia's war against Ukraine.

IN SUMMARY

Extremism is a state of psychological imbalance in which one thing, passion or *idée fixe* dominates the person's concerns to the exclusion of nearly all else. Extremism can bear positive social consequences (as exemplified by Gandhi's contributions to India and the world) but it can also be destructive and cause death and devastation (as exemplified by bin Laden's impact on international terrorism). Not all extremists achieve fame and notoriety (like Gandhi or bin Laden), yet nearly all cause social isolation of the individual, often arising from the individual's unique characteristics. Because humans are quintessentially social beings, the isolation extremists experience can be hard to bear. That is why most forms of extremism are rare, short-lived, and prevalent only in small minorities of the population, possibly individuals with an "extreme personality." A major way of overcoming social isolation is becoming a leader of a movement committed to the leader's extreme ideas, or joining an existing group of similarly minded others already devoted to those ideas. And a major way of bringing the extremist back into the fold of the mainstream is offering them acceptance and support within that fold. That means a "big tent" orientation focused on inclusiveness of the mainstream and support for diversity.

NOTES

1   Moskalenko, S., & McCauley, C. (2019). *Marvel of martyrdom*. Oxford University Press

2   Bicchieri, C., Dimant, E., Gächter, S., Nosenzo, D., & Starmer, C. (2018). Are theories of reciprocal cooperation with complete information realistic? Experimental evidence. *Games and Economic Behavior*, 112, 101–119. https://doi.org/10.1016/j.geb.2018.09.008; Rutkowski, G. K., Gruder, C. L., & Romer, D. (1983). Group cohesiveness, social norms, and bystander intervention. *Journal of Personality and Social Psychology*, 44(3), 545–552. https://doi.org/10.1037/0022-3514.44.3.545

3   Fehr, E., & Fischbacher, U. (2004). Third-party punishment and social norms. *Evolution and Human Behavior*, 25, 63–87. https://doi.org/10.2139/ssrn.495443; Posner, R. A., Rasmusen, E., Ellickson, R. C., McAdams, R. H., McGinnis, M. D., & Ramseyer, J. M. (1999). Creating and enforcing norms, with special reference to sanctions. *International Review of Law and Economics*, 99(3), 435–5806. https://doi.org/10.1016/s0144-8188(99)00013-7; Schunk, D., & Wagner, V. (2021). What determines the willingness to sanction violations of newly introduced social norms: Personality traits or economic preferences? Evidence from the COVID-19 crisis. *Journal of Behavioral and Experimental Economics*, 93, 101716. https://doi.org/10.1016/j.socec.2021.101716

4   Potembska, E., & Pawłowska, B. A. (2012). Symptoms of mobile phone addiction in Polish adolescents at risk and at no risk of internet addiction. *European Psychiatry*, 27(1), 77. https://doi.org/10.1016/S0924-9338(12)74244-X

5   Mentzoni, R. A., Brunborg, G. S., Molde, H., Myrseth, H., Skouverøe, K. J. M., Hetland, J., & Pallesen, S. (2011). Problematic video game use: Estimated prevalence and associations with mental and physical health. *Cyberpsychology, Behavior, and Social Networking*, 14(10), 591–596. https://doi.org/10.1089/cyber.2010.0260; Wenzel, H. G., Bakken, I. J., Johansson, A., Götestam, K. G., & Øren, A. (2009). Excessive computer game playing among Norwegian adults: Self-reported consequences of playing and association with mental health problems. *Psychological Reports*, 105(3), 1237–1247. https://doi.org/10.2466/pr0.105.3.1237-1247

6   Veale, D. C. (1987). Exercise dependence. *British Journal of Addiction*, 82(7), 735–740. https://doi.org/10.1111/j.1360-0443.1987.tb01539.x; Szabo, A. (2000). Physical activity as a source of psychological dysfunction. In S. J. Biddle, K. R. Fox, & S. H. Boutcher (Eds.), *Physical activity and psychological wellbeing* (pp. 130–153). Routledge.

7 Terry, A., Szabo, A., & Griffiths, M. (2004). The exercise addiction inventory: A new brief screening tool. *Addiction Research & Theory*, 12(5), 489–499. https://doi.org/10.1080/16066350310001637363

8 Terry, A., Szabo, A., & Griffiths, M. (2004). The exercise addiction inventory: A new brief screening tool. *Addiction Research & Theory*, 12(5), 489–499. https://doi.org/10.1080/16066350310001637363

9 Attia, E., & Walsh, B. T. (2009). Behavioral management for anorexia nervosa. *The New England Journal of Medicine*, 360(5), 500–506. https://doi.org/10.1056/NEJMct0805569; Hoek, H. W. (2006). Incidence, prevalence and mortality of anorexia nervosa and other eating disorders. *Current Opinion in Psychiatry*, 19, 389–394. https://doi.org/10.1097/01.yco.0000228759.95237.78; Hudson, J. I., Hiripi, E., Pope, H. G., & Kessler, R. C. (2007). The prevalence and correlates of eating disorders in the national comorbidity survey replication. *Biological Psychiatry*, 61(3), 348–358. https://doi.org/10.1016/j.biopsych.2006.03.040; Leon, G. R., Fulkerson, J. A., Perry, C. L., & Cudeck, R. (1993). Personality and behavioral vulnerabilities associated with risk status for eating disorders in adolescent girls. *Journal of Abnormal Psychology*, 102(3), 438–444. https://doi.org/10.1037//0021-843x.102.3.438; Smink, F. R. E., van Hoeken, D., & Hoek, H. W. (2012). Epidemiology of eating disorders: Incidence, prevalence and mortality rates. *Current Psychiatry Reports*, 14(4), 406–414. https://doi.org/10.1007/s11920-012-0282-y; Striegel-Moore, R. H., & Franko, D. L. (2003). Epidemiology of binge eating disorder. *International Journal of Eating Disorders*, 34(S1), S19–S29. https://doi.org/10.1002/eat.10202

10 Bushnell, J. A., Wells, J. E., Hornblow, A. R., Oakley-Browne, M. A., & Joyce, P. (1990). Prevalence of three bulimia syndromes in the general population. *Psychological Medicine*, 20(3), 671–680. https://doi.org/10.1017/S0033291700017190; Fairburn, C. G., & Beglin, S. J. (1990). Studies of the epidemiology of bulimia nervosa. *American Journal of Psychiatry*, 147(4), 401–408. https://doi.org/10.1176/ajp.147.4.401; Heatherton, T. F., Mahamedi, F., Striepe, M., Field, A. E., & Keel, P. (1997). A 10-year longitudinal study of body weight, dieting, and eating disorder symptoms. *Journal of Abnormal Psychology*, 106(1), 117–125. https://doi.org/10.1037//0021-843x.106.1.117

11 Hoek, H. W. (2006). Incidence, prevalence and mortality of anorexia nervosa and other eating disorders. *Current Opinion in Psychiatry*, 19, 389–394. https://doi.org/10.1097/01.yco.0000228759.95237.78

12 Umasy, N. (n.d.). *Woz's Blue boxes*. HistoryMaps. https://history-maps.com/story/Steve-Jobs/event/Woz's-Blue-Boxes

13 Young, J. S. (1987). *Steve Jobs: The journey is the reward* (Amazon Digital Services, 2011 ebook edition). Scott Foresman.

14 Plafke, J. (2011, October 12). Steve Jobs wore turtlenecks because Sony had a uniform code. *The Mary Sue*. https://www.themarysue.com/why-steve-jobs-wore-turtlenecks/

15 Brucculieri, J. (2019, March 20). What to know about Issey Miyake, the man behind Elizabeth Holmes' turtlenecks. *HuffPost*. https://www.huffpost.com/entry/issey-miyake-elizabeth-holmes-black-turtleneck_l_5c925110e4b0dbf58e46bfcc

16 Isaacson, W. (2011). *Steve jobs* (Google Book version). Simon & Schuster. https://doi.org/10.17231/comsoc.22(2012).1283

17 Dahl, M. (2011, November 2). The strange eating habits of Steve Jobs. *NBC News*. https://www.nbcnews.com/health/body-odd/strange-eating-habits-steve-jobs-f119434

18 Stanford Report. (2005, June 12). You've got to find what you love. *Jobs Says*. https://news.stanford.edu/2005/06/12/youve-got-find-love-jobs-says/

19 Weiner, E. (2016, March 11). Gastronomy of genius: History's great minds and the foods that fueled them. NPR. https://www.npr.org/sections/thesalt/2016/03/11/469543237/the-gastronomy-of-genius-food-and-drink-that-inspired-great-minds

20 Rood, R. (2012, February 20). "'Does he eat and drink and sleep? Is he like other men?'" – Newton, by Peter Ackroyd. *Books to the Ceiling*. https://robertarood.wordpress.com/2008/09/15/does-he-eat-and-drink-and-sleep-is-he-like-other-men-newton-by-peter-ackrotd/

3

ASSESSING YOUR OWN EXTREMISM

People differ in their propensity to extremism. You might have noticed it yourself in some of your friends, colleagues, or family members. Is any of them more than the others known for their single-mindedness, the ability to focus on one thing to the exclusion of anything else? Remember that being an extremist as such is neither good nor bad; the tendency to display a "one track mind" can be used for constructive pursuits (devotion to art, to science, or to a worthy humanitarian cause) but also for destructive ones as illustrated by the following true story.

Some years ago, in Sri Lanka, we interviewed an officer of the Sri Lankan military who dealt with the detained members of the extremist organization Liberation Tigers of Tamil Eelam (LTTE), and especially with the suicide squads of that organization known as "Black Tigers." This officer told us an intriguing story about how the LTTE have been selecting people for that suicidal unit viewed as heroic, and hence highly prestigious. The selection procedure, apparently, went like this. Before the critical interview, the candidate was ushered into a waiting room where they were to spend about 20 minutes. The waiting room was appointed with various items of furniture but also with paintings, posters, a calendar, and other items. Upon subsequently being called in to the interviewer's office, the

DOI: 10.4324/9781003472476-3

first question put to the candidate was what objects they noticed in the waiting room. One would have thought that remembering lots of objects, attesting to the candidate's power of observation would be an advantage, and that a candidate who did well in this regard would have a greater chance of being selected, right? Wrong. The logic of the selection procedure was the very opposite! In fact, it privileged candidates who remember very little, nearly nothing about the waiting room. Why, we asked. The reason, the officer said, was that candidates whose mind wandered, noticing things in the waiting room, weren't sufficiently focused on the idea of becoming a suicide attacker; hence, they weren't sufficiently committed. Only those candidates who could apparently think of nothing else but their wish to join the squad were selected. These were the kinds of people who would be able to shut out thoughts that might interfere with the mission, thoughts about the family they were leaving behind, their jobs and hobbies, beautiful nature around them, life itself. These were the kind of people whose personality predisposed them to be successful extremists, and that is why they were chosen for this most extreme mission of all, where they would be required to sacrifice their lives for a cause.

THE EXTREMISM SCALE

Though the LTTE method of identifying would-be extremists is inventive, there is an easier, and more efficient way of doing so. It is made possible, fortunately, by the creative and extensive work of Dr Ewa Szumowska of the Jagiellonian University in the Polish city of Krakow. The construction of the scale by Dr Szumowska's team was a laborious affair. After all, the idea that people differ in their propensity toward extremism and that a person who is extreme in one domain (say, eating) is also more likely to be extreme in another domain (e.g. their political preferences) is a new and surprising one. Therefore, a great deal of effort was required to construct a scale that would measure people's tendency toward extremism in a valid and reliable fashion.

To those ends, researchers conducted 19 studies that included 8,018 participants. These studies demonstrated that the scale is reliable; that it measures a personality trait (a tendency toward extremity) that is stable over time; and that it is valid.

The demonstration of validity was accomplished by showing that the scale was "diagnostic": it predicted engagement in extreme behaviors in very different domains, including extreme dieting, extreme religious practices, extreme romantic behaviors, extreme self-sacrifice, addictive behaviors, extreme fandom, extreme activism, and obsessive passion for a hobby or interest.

Recall that our theory of extremism assumes that in an extreme state of mind one privileges a given concern above all the others. Under these conditions, one is then ready to do anything to address their primary concern, no matter the cost. What this means is that for a person in such state of mind *anything goes* that promises to satisfy that concern. If so, persons who achieve a high score on the scale of extremism should report using a greater number of strategies than less extreme persons. And indeed, this is exactly what the research has found. In addition, individuals whom most people would regard as extremists should obtain higher scores than ones we would consider as moderates. This hypothesis was also supported. Extreme dieters scored higher than non-extreme dieters; people who engage in extreme sports (bungee jumping, helicopter skiing) scored higher than people who engage in less extreme sports. People who engage in extreme sexual practices, members of the Bondage, Discipline, Dominance, Submission, Sadism, and Masochism (BDSM) community, scored higher on the extremism scale than did people that engaged in more mainstream sexual practices. Similarly, extreme environmental activists scored higher on the scale than less extreme activists.

Our psychological theory of extremism suggests also that people who obtain high scores on the scale will have more volatile emotional lives than the low scorers. Because the extremists put "all their eggs in one basket"; they are extremely happy when they succeed in addressing that concern (when their "basket" is safe and sound), and extremely unhappy when they fail to do so (when their "basket" is compromised). Indeed, Dr Szumowska finds in her studies that people who score high on the extremism scale report greater emotional peaks and valleys (ups and downs) than do the low scorers. All in all, the results of the extensive research conducted on the scale shows that it has highly satisfying properties as a measuring instrument of people's personal tendency toward extremism. It suggests that there is indeed such a thing as an "extreme personality." People differ in their proneness to motivational imbalance, which underlies diverse extreme behaviors. Moreover, these results suggest that the same psychological makeup, or core dynamic, can underlie very different types of extremism, including engagement in anti-social actions on the one hand and highly pro-social, humanistic action on the other hand.

If you are curious about your own results on the extremism scale, here is a great opportunity to find out where you stand in comparison with thousands of individuals from around the world who have filled it out before. Keep in mind that the score, whatever it is, says nothing about your level of happiness, achievement, popularity, or intelligence. The scale measures one thing, namely your tendency to be extreme in pursuits of things and ideas that interest you, to develop a "one-track mind" and tend to forget, discount or disregard other things and pursuits.

THE SCALE ITEMS

And here are the instructions about responding to the scale and the specific scale items that tap the respondent's tendency toward the extreme:

"Below, we will ask you about your thoughts, feelings, and behaviors related to goal pursuit. In each statement, please select an answer that describes you best."

Be honest—there are no right or wrong answers!

1.   Definitely disagree

2. Disagree
3. Slightly disagree
4. Definitely neither agree nor disagree
5. Slightly agree
6. Agree
7. Definitely agree

1. My life is usually dominated by one main pursuit/desire.
2. I usually invest all of my time and energy into the one thing that matters to me the most.
3. I spend most of my time thinking about the one goal that matters to me the most.
4. Typically, my happiness depends on the one thing that I value most.
5. When I devote myself to a goal, everything else becomes insignificant.
6. There is usually one goal that looms large in my mind.
7. My entire life is often subordinated to the one thing I find most important.
8. Typically, there is only one thing that can make me happy in life.
9. I stay faithful to my most important goal, even when it requires sacrifices to my other goals.
10. When I decide on something, I go for it like my life depended on it.
11. When I focus on my most important goal, I easily forget other things.
12. I react very emotionally to anything that is related to my most important goal.

Scoring the scale

Scoring the extremism scale should be an easy affair. Each question is scored on a one to seven rating scale (from 1 = Definitely Disagree to 7 = Definitely Agree). Each numerical response to the scale's questions is than added; the total sum is the scale score. A person who scores between 63 and 84 is pretty high on their personal predilection toward extremism. Such person's scores fall in the upper quarter of the possible extremism values. A person who scores between 12 and 21 is low on extremism as their scores fall in the lower quarter of possible scale values. And finally, a person whose scores fall between 21 and 63 is intermediate on extremism, such that the higher their scores within that range the more they tend toward extremism, and the lower their score within that range the more they tend toward moderation.

WHAT DOES IT MEAN?

Diagnosing yourself or your friends' tendencies toward extremism can be quite telling about major aspects of personality, one's feelings in response to successes and failures, about social connections, and about the challenges and difficulties on one's path. People who score high on the extremism scale tend to experience their successes and/or failures acutely. Their emotional lives are often characterized by more intense and pronounced ups and downs than those of more moderate people. Also, because of their tendency to focus on one thing to the exclusion of other pursuits, they may at times feel isolated and different from other people, even from their families and friends. For the same reason, too, people who score high on the extremism scale tend to neglect or sacrifice other aspects of their lives. Their extremism may also incur costs from downplaying other basic needs. Some extremists may neglect their health, personal relations, their professional commitments—and suffer in consequence. At the same time, extremists can succeed where moderate individuals would have long given up, defying the odds and persevering despite formidable obstacles. Whatever the goal, whether it is professional success, athletic performance, academic achievement, or indeed violent and destructive pursuits such as terrorism, hoarding, or dogged pursuit of raw power and dominance, extremists are more likely to attain it than non-extremists.

Scoring at the other end of the scale, in the lower quartile of the possible scores, may also have its drawbacks. It may reflect a lower ability to commit to an idea or a person, an absence of grit necessary for most worthwhile accomplishments and achievements. The upside to the opposite of extremism is possibly the kind of outlook that allows one to exist outside of life's struggles, where nothing bothers them too much, where they can "take it or leave it," be content with being instead of doing, enjoying every day for everything it has to offer instead of pursuing an agenda. The middle scorers, on the other hand, are often blessed with the most harmonious existence. They can commit to a project and pursue it relentlessly, but also recognize when enough is enough and when their "idée fixe" demands of them more than it's worth in the larger scheme of things.

THE BENEFITS OF SELF-KNOWLEDGE

The advice to "Know Thyself" was inscribed above the entrance to the temple of Apollo at Delphi, site of the sacred oracle whom the people of Greece would visit to find out what fate awaited them, or what course of action to take in different choice points of their lives. Modern science of psychology offers a different path to self-knowledge through meticulously validated measuring instruments like the extreme personality scale above. This scale does not pretend to foretell your future or divine the secrets of your destiny—it may teach you a thing or two about yourself that can be helpful.

For instance, finding out that you are an "extremist" based on a high score you received on the extremism scale would provide an explanation for your behavioral and emotional reactions to people and events that may have been puzzling for you otherwise. How you are able to be single-minded for the object of your passion, how you suffer when your pursuits go awry, and how intensely euphoric you feel when they succeed. Knowing these things about yourself and how they go together may also throw light on your relations with other people who may not be as committed and single-minded about things as are you.

On the other hand, finding out that you score low on the extremism scale can also be illuminating. You may realize that it is your reluctance to go all out after the objects of your desire that is holding you back in professional life or in interpersonal relations.

Whether your score is high or low, it offers two kinds of possibilities. One has to with changing your extremist tendencies toward greater moderation. If you find that high extremism is causing you too much stress, that you miss out on life's important milestones and experiences because you're too focused on your single-minded pursuit, you may wish to tamper your extremism. Or you may feel that you are too laid back, and wish to move a bit more toward extremism in order to achieve important goals.

The other possibility has to do not with the degree but with kind of extremism you might pursue. Suppose you score high on extremism scale, and that suits you just fine. You like to reap the benefits of dogged determination that's part of your personality. In this case, knowing your score may alert you to a vulnerability: where someone moderate can safely navigate certain environments, you might want to be especially judicious not to fall into a trap of destructive extremism, by deciding early on what your "stopping points" are, and committing to them with the same dedication as you tend to commit to other goals. For example, if the social media tend to suck you in for hours on end, you may wish to program (reasonable) daily limits on your devices, and stick with them; or if you tend to spend days and nights on a hobby skipping meals and barely sleeping, you may wish to set routine alarms every day to take time away from your extreme pursuit for physical activity or to socialize.

Later in the book, we will have more to say about both: how to reduce or increase own extremism, and how to direct it away from destructive and toward constructive pursuits. In either case, you may be perfectly happy with the way you are (whether high or low on the propensity toward extremism) and may wish to keep things as they are, or you might be unwilling to pay the price of too much or too little extremism. Such insights could be the first step toward initiating change: teaching yourself to curb your enthusiasms if they tend to be hurtful to you or to people you care about, or, to the contrary, learn to allow yourself to sometimes go out on a limb for what's important to you.

IN SUMMARY

This chapter offers readers an opportunity to assess their own propensity toward extremism via a psychological measure of extremism. This well-validated scale assesses one's tendency to focus exclusively on a given dominant concern, and sacrifice other basic concerns for it. Assessing one's own proclivity toward extremism allows a personal connection to the discussions of diverse aspects of extremism. It will also help one determine whether to modify (e.g. tone down or perhaps turn up) one's degree of extremism.

4

EXTREMISM THEN AND NOW

It might seem as though extremism is a unique trademark of our times. But there is nothing new under the sun, and extremism is neither a novel nor a Western phenomenon. It is part of our human nature, a potential inherent in each and every one of us, if not to the same degree. Ancient mythologies from around the world depict extremism in various forms.

Extreme gluttony, for instance, was represented by deities around the world and throughout human history. Chinese Taotie is said to be a monster of insatiable appetite, devouring everything and everyone in its path, leaving only the heads of its victims behind.[1] Its prehistoric depictions portray a beast with bulging eyes and a gaping mouth. Ancient Philistines believed in a demon of gluttony Beelzebub,[2] also known as Lord of Flies, because he could fly and expel swarms of flies who feasted on anything and everything. Later religious traditions portrayed Beelzebub under different names, such as Beelzebul, who in Hebrew tradition is said to cause destruction through tyrants, to cause demons to be worshipped by men, to inspire lust in priests, to cause jealousies, murders, and war. This broader interpretation echoes the idea of extreme gluttony, which was the original power of Beelzebul.

DOI: 10.4324/9781003472476-4

THE TOLL

Ancient Greek mythology tells the story of King Midas who ruled over the country of Phrygia. His tale highlights the price extremism can exact. Midas had every luxury he desired, but so extreme was his love for money that he spent his days counting gold coins in his coffers, and covering his entire body in gold jewelry and ornaments. One day, the Greek god of wine and parties, Dionisius, was passing through Midas' kingdom. A favorite Satyr of Dionisius, Silenus, got lost in the wilderness and was rescued by Midas, who brought him back to Dionisius. In gratitude, the god offered to grant Midas any wish. "I want everything I touch to turn into gold," said the greedy king. Dionisius, being a god, and possibly having a broader perspective on things for that reason, warned Midas to think twice about his wish. But when an extremist is after something, reasoning is unlikely to sway them. And so Dionisius granted Midas his wish, effective the following day.

The next morning, Midas woke up eager to multiply his riches: first, he touched a small stone—and voila, it turned into gold! Midas then touched a table, then a chair, a carpet—and everything immediately became gold. He spent some time turning things within reach into gold, delighting ever more with every touch, until he grew tired and decided to eat a grape. But as soon as he touched it, it turned to gold just as Dionisius had promised. Midas touched a slice of bread, a glass of water, and realized why Dionisius had suggested he think twice about his wish. The king's daughter entered the room just as Midas was sinking into despair, and he rushed into her embrace hoping to find solace, only to turn his beloved daughter into a gold statue. This is when the full horror of his predicament hit Midas, and he prayed to Dionisius to take away this gift which turned into a curse. The god took pity on Midas, relieved him of the "Midas touch," and turned his daughter back to human form. From that point on, Midas left his extremism behind, became generous with his people, and grateful for all life had to offer, not just riches. His kingdom prospered as a result, and when he died his people mourned him as a beloved ruler. The cautionary tale of King Midas has a happy ending.

The Midas story is no mere moralistic sermon about the sinfulness of avarice; it also conveys the psychological wisdom that every extremism creates a gap, a deprivation that undermines the extremist's wellbeing. By focusing on gold to the exclusion of all else, Midas nearly sacrificed his own life and died of hunger or thirst while also causing the demise of his beloved daughter. By channeling all their mental energies into a single concern, the extremists drain resources from their remaining needs, so these no longer seem to matter. They then become prone to deny them (as in Midas' case), ultimately causing themselves torment and misery.

OVERSHOOTING

Because of their deprivation-induced suffering, extremists rarely stay long in their exaggerated state. Some, like King Midas, learn their lesson and retreat to moderation. Others might "overshoot" on their way out of extremism right past moderation and into a different kind of extremism, often the polar opposite of the original. Their attempt to address a previously neglected topic or concern turns into obsession. In his celebrated 1951 book *The True Believer*, philosopher Eric Hoffer discusses cases of devoted communists becoming adamant fascists, religious fanatics reinventing themselves as committed atheists and vice versa. And there are real-life examples of people who, like King Midas, abandoned their relentless pursuit of wealth and embraced spirituality and the service to others with the same relentless fervor as they used to devote to riches. Consider, for example, Bhanwarlal Doshi, a son of a textile merchant in India, who started his business—trading raw plastic materials—with a loan of about $400 from his father, and grew an empire worth $100 million, earning him the title "Plastic King" of Delhi.[3] At the age of 58, however, the Plastic King gave up his riches and his lavish lifestyle to become a Jain monk.

Likewise, Liu Jingchong was a multimillionaire in China, a successful manufacturing and textile baron, when he gave up all his luxuries in favor of a minimalist lifestyle at the age 39.[4] He sold his possessions, cars, and homes, and bought a small hut in a remote area. After two years in isolation in the mountains, where he spent almost no money, slept on a bed of bricks, and rose with the sun, Jingchong came across a monk, and followed him to a temple in Eastern China, where he now works in the communal kitchen.

Venerable Ajahn Siripanyo was not only the son of Malaysia's third-richest person, worth reportedly $5 billion, but Thai royalty on his mother's side. He gave up all of that to become a Buddhist monk and live in obscurity and poverty.[5]

Perhaps less dramatically than giving up their entire fortune, self-made billionaires often turn to philanthropy, giving away the money they were so doggedly accumulating in the extremist period of their career. Bill Gates, the co-founder of software giant Microsoft and the richest man on Earth every year from 1995 to 2017, has donated sizable amounts of money through the Bill & Melinda Gates Foundation, the world's largest private charity. Among the foundation's better-known causes are vaccination campaigns that contributed to the eradication of the polio virus and tackled malaria in Africa. Gates also co-founded with Warren Buffet The Giving Pledge, an initiative through which other billionaires can pledge to give at least half of their wealth to philanthropy.[6] So it seems that extreme wealth accumulation can occasionally be reversed, leading the individual formerly focused exclusively on getting to turn instead to giving.

EXTREMISM'S BENEFITS

Though extremism is fraught with deprivation, it often gets the job done; on balance, therefore, it may be considered necessary and well worth the price in some circumstances. Artists like Vincent Van Gogh, scientists like Marie Sklodowska-Curie, religious martyrs like Jesus, or revolutionary leaders like Gandhi or Martin Luther King were known for their single-minded extremism. Caution and risk aversion may only get one so far; sometimes it is incumbent to put all of one's eggs in one basket, and risk it all. In fact, we all are prone to become extremists in situations of danger and emergency, to cast everything aside to meet the challenge.

Ancient myths and legends colorfully depict this dynamic. The Hindu goddess Kali is said to have been born out of wrath when goddess Durga was attacked. Durga's anger caused her face to turn dark, and Kali appeared out of Durga's forehead, with dark blue skin, gaunt red eyes, and a garland of human skulls around her neck. Kali defeated Durga's attackers, and later defeated a monster Raktabija who cloned himself with every drop of his spilled blood. Kali sucked his blood before it could be spilled, and ate the numerous clones. Extreme anger can be very useful when battling monsters, as Kali's story demonstrates—even if it comes with the side-effects of gaunt red eyes, blue skin, and disturbing eating habits.

EXTREMISM LOVES COMPANY

Because it entails sacrifices, extremism is difficult to endure. Therefore, most people avoid extremism and opt for moderation. For the same reason, instances of extremism have been typically short-lived. Extreme dieting, engagement in extreme sports, or addiction to video games typically does not last very long.[7] This circumstance can change if one has access to fellow extremists who share one's passion and support it. If that happens, a shared reality is created in which extremism is the new normal. The Israeli terrorism expert, Ariel Merari, in his 2010 book *Driven to Death*, describes how Palestinians designated to become suicide bombers are generally kept together and are prevented from contact with others outside their circle, including their families. Such isolation creates a protected cognitive enclave in which the narrative that extols dying for a cause is embraced by all, facing no competition from alternative, life-affirming, narratives.

The proliferation of social media drastically reduced the difficulty of creating a protected cognitive space for extreme ideas. No matter how esoteric, strange, or deviant is one's worldview, it is easy enough to find on the internet similarly minded others and create an "echo chamber." Moreover, the crowded social media environment creates incentives for extremism. In today's overpopulated, globalized, and ever-more-competitive environment that we access through the screens of our phones or computers, to stand out one must embark on extremism of some sort—or risk blending in and falling behind. Stories of others' achievements abound—and not just "your mother's friend's kid" but stories of kids around the world—are flaunted on the internet as anxiety-evoking comparisons. Seeking a place under the sun in this jungle, the odds stacking higher and higher against us, we strive for extraordinary heights. The temperate olden days might have been captured by the expressions "for better or worse" and "fair-to-middling." But that just won't cut it in today's rat race. "Publish or perish" and "funny or die" are the new normal.

SOCIAL FACILITATION

Social psychology offers experimental paradigms to help us understand how social media might contribute to extremism. Consider, for example, the Social Facilitation effect, studied by Robert Zajonc.[8] If you are a runner, you probably have a time and place where you like to run. At times, you might see nobody while running; but what happens when there is a person looking in your direction—or running alongside you? Do you run at the same speed then as you do when running alone? Social facilitation research suggests that the "mere presence" of an observer would make you run faster. That just having someone look at you while you are performing a well-practiced task makes you give it more effort. The reason, Zajonc found, was "evaluation apprehension"—when a runner realizes they are visible and therefore could be judged on running performance, they boost performance, giving a little more of their resources to the task at hand, moving a little toward the extreme as a result of someone watching them. This effect is not exclusive to physical resources, either: people give more of their monetary resources when they are observed while donating to a charitable cause,[9] also moving a little more toward the extreme in their altruism than they may be naturally inclined.

With social media holding a viewing lens into our lives to countless people, friends and strangers alike, it is easy for evaluation apprehension to set in. Depending on how engaged one is with Instagram, TikTok, Snapchat, Facebook, or X, one's entire life may seem as though it is being watched. As a result, they might give more and more of their resources, moving more to the extreme, to present to others an "enhanced" version of themselves.

But people on social media are not "just" watching us. They tend to compete with us—as we do with them. Posting photos from an exotic vacation spot shows off one's worldliness; a post about a child's admission into a prestigious college parades parenting successes, a flattering selfie showcases one's good looks—and all of this, however implicitly, is to compete with one's group of "friends" or "followers." Competition is social facilitation on steroids. Whereas a runner speeds up at the sight of an observer by their track, they run even faster than that if another runner catches up with them.[10]

COMPETITION ASCENDING

A famous experiment demonstrated the effects of competition on extremism "in the wild"—at the Robbers Cave State Park, in Oklahoma.[11] Psychologist Muzafer Sherif created a summer sleepaway camp in the park, and invited 20 psychologically normal tween boys to spend three weeks there. Potential campers were tested on a variety of psychological measures to make sure they were not particularly violent or troubled. Unbeknownst to them, the boys were randomly divided into one of two groups and stationed at campsites far enough away from one another that they could remain ignorant of the other team's presence for a while. Sherif observed how each group socialized, including emerging leadership hierarchies and social norms (for example, one group of boys discouraged rough language, the other quite embraced it). After each group evolved into a cohesive social unit, Sherif orchestrated for the two groups to run into each other—at a baseball diamond that each group had thought was exclusively theirs. Sherif staged competitions between the groups, such as games of tug of war, and relays—with coveted prizes for the winning team. The result of this carefully curated competition was increasing extremism and hostility between the two groups of boys. They called the other team names (such as "pigs" or "stinkers"), raided the other team's bunkhouse, burned the other's flag. At a picnic where both groups ate together, a food fight broke out. In other words, competition alone was enough to foster extremism and even violence among normal, not especially aggressive boys.

Not to worry: Sherif did not end the study there, leaving the boys in their newly evolved state of extremism. To reduce hostility, he introduced "superordinate goals"—goals that the two groups shared and had to work together to achieve. First, Sherif compromised the camp's water supply, causing the two teams of boys to seek a solution and eventually to discover that it could only be attained when they pooled their resources. Next, the food truck that was bringing provisions for both groups just happened to "get stuck" in the mud en route to the camp. To get it out of the rut, all the boys had to work together to push and pull. This and other cooperative efforts had the effect Sherif predicted, namely the boys becoming friendlier toward the other group, and the hostilities giving way to friendships across what used to be enemy lines.

Extremism is about scale: being the best, the brightest, the strongest, having the most of something or the least of something. It is, therefore, often about competition.[12] Competing against two people, the odds of winning are 1:3. Competing against three thousand people, the odds are a thousand times lower, the competition is a thousand times steeper, and the effort required to attain the desired high status must be that much greater.

Fifty years ago, teenage girls had only their classmates and neighbors to compete with on "who's the prettiest of them all." But Instagram changed that. Suddenly, the referent group expanded by hundreds of thousands around the world. And the result of using Instagram for many young women was comparing themselves with others whose images they saw on the social media site, feeling more dissatisfied with their own bodies and wanting to be thinner.[13] The more girls and young women used Instagram, research found, the more dissatisfied they were with their appearance, resulting in more depression and anxiety.[14] Perhaps not surprisingly, frequent use of social media among adolescents (both boys and girls) was significantly correlated with extreme thoughts and behaviors intended to cause weight loss, such as "made myself vomit (throw up)," "ate very little food" and "skipped meals."[15]

Young people are not the only ones who get pushed into extremism by social media. During the COVID-19 pandemic, the US government instituted mandatory lockdowns, forcing millions of people into isolation. For many, the only window into the world during this time was through their computers. Chapter 2 suggested that social isolation can be a cause or a correlate of extremism: without the normalizing influence of non-extreme people, nothing tampers the budding extremist tendencies, allowing them to blossom. For millions of Americans, the isolation of COVID lockdowns was the medium that allowed their extremism to grow, and the internet generously provided the seeds of extremism in the form of outlandish tales of conspiracy theories and threats. With little available information about the deadly virus, feeling helpless, insecure, and diminished, people searched for ways of regaining their self-confidence and the sense of mattering. Often, the social media's algorithms, designed to maximize engagement, quickly landed users inquiring about "covid virus" or "lockdowns" or "covid vaccines" on internet pages dedicated to spreading disinformation and conspiracy theories. The most notorious conglomerate of conspiracy theories became known as QAnon.[16] The letter Q in QAnon stands for the highest level of US government clearance—an anonymous poster signed by this letter their cryptic messages about worldwide sinister plots by nefarious actors, implying they had privileged information about impending threats. Q's hints and innuendoes invited a following that during COVID lockdowns swelled to tens of millions believers in the USA alone.

The QAnon conspiracy theory claimed that a cabal of Satan-worshipping pedophiles controls the US government and the media, and its members include Tom Hanks, Lady Gaga, the Democratic party leaders like Bill and Hillary Clinton and Nancy Pelosi, billionaires like George Soros and Bill Gates, and even the Pope. According to QAnon, the cabal secretly kidnapped children to torture and sexually abuse them, and to drink their blood for the magic properties it gained as a result of the children's horrific suffering. COVID, according to QAnon, was a hoax orchestrated by the cabal to run their scheme with impunity. Or maybe it was a biological weapon designed by Bill Gates to cause infertility. Or maybe not to cause infertility, but to kill off a large number of people while human–lizard hybrids take over the world. COVID vaccines, QAnon claimed, were either tracking devices, or they were going to cause children to turn into LGBTQ. Or maybe they were poison. Or they were useless, just a ploy by the Big Pharma to enrich itself at everyone's expense. The narratives overlapped and contradicted one another, they multiplied and evolved into an illogical and unfalsifiable narrative reminiscent of psychotic delirium as QAnon followers "did their own research" and "connected the dots."

Although entertaining for us (in the same ways that horror movies and train wrecks can be), these conspiratorial narratives became an overwhelming obsession for many QAnon followers, who spent days and nights in front of their screens, neglecting loved ones and drifting away from their families as their views grew progressively more extreme.[17] Inspired by their QAnon's beliefs, some attacked and killed their own children because they thought the children were lizard people, or because they thought the children were destined for the cabal's torture and would be better off dead.[18]

On January 6, 2021, hundreds of people, many of them QAnon followers, traveled to the Washington, DC, Capitol building, believing that the presidential election was stolen from Donald Trump (in QAnon's narrative, a heroic figure who secretly fights the cabal), hoping to restore Trump to power and to participate in a public execution of the cabal members. Two women who died in the attempted insurrection, Roseanne Boyland and Ashley Babbit, were both fervent believers in QAnon conspiracy theories. Their extreme beliefs contributed to one of the most disturbing political events in American history, and to their own untimely deaths.

Extreme beliefs in QAnon conspiracy theories had other destructive effects. QAnon followers who believed COVID was a hoax refused to wear masks and observe other recommended measures to mitigate the spread of the virus. Those who believed COVID vaccines were poison or tracking devices refused to get them, and prevented their loved ones, especially children, from getting the vaccines. The number of preventable COVID-related deaths among unvaccinated adults alone is estimated at 232,000 in the USA.[19] This number does not include deaths among children, or among those vaccinated adults (possibly immunocompromised) who contracted the virus from the unvaccinated conspiracists and died as a result. It also does not include those who did not die but suffered severe health consequences as a result of getting ill with COVID they contracted because QAnon believers refused to mask or vaccinate. In short, the extreme beliefs of QAnon followers, however unrelated to reality, had very real and tragic consequences for hundreds of thousands of people. These beliefs, which turned into a political movement and a health hazard for the entire country, evolved almost exclusively online, as a result of virtual discussions among people who never met in person.

POLARIZATION

In social psychology, the paradigm that helps understand how extreme beliefs can evolve online is called Group Polarization.

Experiments that demonstrate it place people into groups and ask them to discuss an issue—let's say how much risk is appropriate for a particular reward. Participants' individual opinions are sampled before the group begins the discussion, so we know where everyone stands at the onset. What Group Polarization experiments find is that as a result of discussion, groups tend to become more extreme in whatever direction their members lean in, on average, before the discussion. If the group members were risk-averse individually, then after discussing the issue they will become even more so. If they were risk-seeking on average, then after discussion they will become more so.

Research shows that polarization of group opinion happens for two reasons. One is social comparison: just as teenage girls on Instagram, we are ever comparing ourselves to others, and inadvertently competing with them, not wanting to fall behind whatever trend the group is on, be it a svelte figure or a risky opinion. The other reason for group polarization in discussion is the emergence of informal opinion leaders that others want to emulate. These happen to be individuals with the most extreme opinions. Queried after the discussion, participants in Group Polarization experiments expressed more admiration for group members who expressed the most extreme opinions. "Imitation is the sincerest form of flattery that mediocrity can pay to greatness," said Oscar Wilde. Wanting to move a little closer to greatness (extremism) and a little farther from mediocrity (normalcy), participants in the experiment shifted their original, less extreme, more mainstream opinion a little bit toward that of the most admired group member, resulting in the whole group shifting toward the extreme.

The two reasons why individuals in groups become more extreme (social comparison, and extreme rhetoric) are tightly related. Groups typically develop norms that members come to agree on. Depending on circumstances, these norms can be militant or peaceful, liberal or conservative, religious or secular, achievement, or justice-oriented, etc. The function of these norms is to define for members how they can attain status or significance, and how they can get respect from their fellow members. This is accomplished by being good group members through conforming to the group's cherished norms. Because acquiring status and significance are basic human needs, people compare and compete on how well they do in this respect. Extreme rhetoric expresses a particularly strong commitment to group norms; by adopting that rhetoric group members claim to be especially devoted group members. This is the secret of their influence; other members then follow their lead and the group as a whole becomes more extreme.

INFLUENCERS

We now have a useful word to describe the opinion leaders online who cause individuals to emulate their extreme behaviors and views: influencers. Like extreme leaders of times past, influencers, too, acquire following and status, yet these days their prestige is additionally boosted by the financial gains their influence earns. For example, Achieng Agutu, the 26-year-old influencer who had about 488,000 followers on Instagram, made over $1 million in her first year as a full-time content creator.[20] *Business Insider* detailed the ways social media influencers can monetize their status: by charging brands to promote their merchandise ($100 for every 10,000 followers), earning commissions on affiliate links (or discount codes) provided by brands to earn a percentage of sales; making profits from selling their own merchandise; and earning a share of revenue for high-performing reels on the social media apps. With incredible stories of influencers' financial success, 86% of young Americans said they want to become a social media influencer.[21] Over half said they would quit their jobs to become an influencer. Three in ten young people said they would pay to become influencers.[22]

But while the benefits of being the loudest voice in the crowd are appealing, the costs are often obscured. Kids trying to become influencers are sometimes bullied by their real-life peers for their online content—with so many kids wanting the coveted influencer status, the competition spills over from online to real life, and many aspiring influencers experience the downside without ever making it to the upside. As one *Vox* article summarized:

> Even though so many kids want to be influencers themselves, they can be incredibly tough on their peers who try to make it happen; whether or not they make it as popular influencers, there is an inevitable emotional toll of constant feedback, both online and off.[23]

And for the followers of the influencer, there are tolls as well. Where the influencer may be strategically monetizing their extreme shopping or extreme thinness, the followers tend to forget the behind-the-scenes incentives and ratchet up extremism of their own to emulate the role model. On TikTok (A video-sharing site with over one billion monthly users), one of the most popular tags was "What I eat in a day," with one eating disorder survivor explaining, "You have very thin people who are literally barely eating. One of the harmful things is the comments section, where the kids say, 'oh you're so skinny, I need to eat less to be like you.'"[24]

The costs of influencer-inspired extremism are not limited to diet. The internet is awash in confessions of individuals who say they became shopaholics because of influencers.[25] Brands gift influencers their products—with the expectation that the followers would buy them. Research shows their calculation is correct: influence marketing is the fastest-growing online customer acquisition method.[26] But what's free for the influencer is not for the follower, and many followers find themselves with mounting credit card debts even as their role models are getting rich.[27]

Because influencers are not experts (they just play them on the internet), their power to convince followers can be quite dangerous, especially when it comes to health recommendations. During COVID, internet influencers pushed what amounted to "snake oils" to protect against the virus.[28] The most notorious of these "panaceas" was ivermectin, an antiparasitic drug sold without a prescription at pet stores. In one video shared with 22,000 followers, a US-based influencer said "Ivermectin doesn't just cure [COVID]... it kills cancer, too."[29] This and similar influencers' messages resulted in scores of people around the world ingesting toxic amounts of the drug that was not helpful for COVID or cancer, but was instead very harmful. World Health Organization reported a surge of ivermectin-related toxicity cases among people who took the drug to treat or prevent COVID, resulting in serious neurological adverse reactions among many, and coma and mortality among some.[30,31]

And perhaps the most troubling kind of internet influencing is the one achieved by terrorists who livestream their mass shooting attacks—like Brenton Tarrant, who fatally shot 51 people in the space of 36 minutes, livestreaming his gruesome terror attack on Christchurch, New Zealand.[32] To be sure, for most people watching this video would be traumatizing rather than inspiring. But remember that opinion leaders in group polarization research were only able to lead the group in the direction it was already leaning in. Among radical individuals and groups who already in some ways supported Tarrant's ideas and even the kind of violence he enacted, he became an influencer, inspiring videogames imitating his attack[33] they can play to virtually emulate his actions.

Other terrorist "influencers" posted manifestos declaring their ideology and justifications for their mass murder, such as Elliot Rodger of Isla Vista, California, who killed six people in a stabbing and shooting spree. In a 141-page manifesto and videos he uploaded online, Rodger explained his violence as a retribution for not being able to find a girlfriend by age 22.[34] Rodger became an "influencer" for an online community of "Incels"—involuntarily celibate men who feel aggrieved about being unable to form romantic relationships. His posts inspired another mass killing by a member of the Incel community, Alek Minassian, who murdered ten people by plowing his van into a crowd in one of Toronto's busiest streets.[35] Research among hundreds of self-identified Incels showed that admiration for Elliot Rodger and for Alek Minassian was predictive of own willingness to "rape if I could get away with it"[36] and other radical intentions, such as attacking police and security forces and breaking laws to advance one's ideology.[37]

Terrorism, political violence, and weaponized misogyny are not new. They have been around for hundreds of years. What is new, however, is how easy it is for extremists of any kind to find likeminded others, form communities, and through online interactions become even more polarized than they were before—by emulating the most extreme and therefore most admired group members. This day and age, for terrorist "influencers," to spread a 141-page manifesto to tens of thousands of people is as easy as clicking a button; to share a video of a murder spree takes only a body cam and access to the internet. And their audiences have likewise expanded exponentially, granting easy access to any kinds of extremist materials.

In short, although extremism may be as old as humanity, we may be living in a unique time when "what's allowed for the Jupiter" is increasingly more accessible, more desirable, and more "allowed for the bull," as well. Not just legendary kings and mythical deities, but girls and boys next door can now vie for extreme beauty, extreme riches, and extreme violence. "Celebrities: they are just like us" used to be a popular section in tabloid magazines. Now, the tables have turned, and we can be just like celebrities—if only we become influential enough by being extreme enough.

IN SUMMARY

The potential for extremism is an inseparable part of human nature. Its presence is attested by ancient myths and historical accounts; it has been shaping the fates of nations and individuals from times immemorial. Then and now, it has been a force whose unleashing can accomplish great things but also can cause suffering and destruction. Though not inherently social, its consequences are especially impactful in social environments where people compete for status and significance. And in our times of unprecedented connectedness and social comparison afforded by technology and social media, the threats of extremism, exaggeration, and polarization pose particularly daunting challenges for individuals and societies around the globe.

NOTES

1 PBS. (2021). Monstrum—*Taotie: The mystery of Chinese mythology's famous glutton* [*Video*]. Twin Cities PBS. https://www.tpt.org/monstrum/video/taotie-the-mystery-of-chinese-mythologys-famous-glutton-xzpbtl/,

2 Freedman, D. N. (Ed.). (1996). Beelzebul. In F. D. Noel (Ed.), *The Anchor Yale Bible dictionary* (Vol. 1, p. 639). Doubleday.

3 Chatterjee, R. (2016, July 15). Bhanwarlal Raghunath Doshi, the millionaire who gave up his empire to become a Jain monk. *HuffPost*. https://www.huffpost.com/archive/in/entry/bhanwarlal-raghunath-doshi-the-millionaire-who-gave-up-his-empi_n_7482218

4 Sumitra. (2015, August 12). Chinese millionaire gives up fortune, lives in isolation for two years to become Buddhist monk. *Oddity Central*. https://www.odditycentral.com/news/chinese-millionaire-gives-up-fortune-lives-in-isolation-for-two-years-to-become-buddhist-monk.html

5 Today Online. (2020, July 27). The billionaire heir who became a monk: Why the son of Malaysia's third-richest man renounced luxury and fortune for spiritual peace. *Today Online*. https://www.todayonline.com/world/billionaire-heir-who-became-monk-why-son-malaysias-third-richest-man-renounced-luxury-and

6 Loomis, C. J. (2016, January 17). The $600 billion challenge. *Fortune*. https://fortune.com/2010/06/16/the-600-billion-challenge/

7 Kruglanski, A. W., Szumowska, E., Kopetz, C. H., Vallerand, R. J., & Pierro, A. (2021). On the psychology of extremism: How motivational imbalance breeds intemperance. *Psychological Review, 128*(2), 264–289. https://doi.org/10.1037/rev0000260

8 Zajonc, R. B. (1965). Social facilitation: A solution is suggested for an old unresolved social psychological problem. *Science, 149*(3681), 269–274.

9 Izuma, K., Saito, D. N., & Sadato, N. (2010). Processing of the incentive for social approval in the ventral striatum during charitable donation. *Journal of Cognitive Neuroscience, 22*(4), 621–631. https://doi.org/10.1162/jocn.2009.21228

10 Chen, P. (2010). *Yin and yang theory of competition: Social comparison and evaluation apprehension reciprocally drive competitive motivation* (Doctoral dissertation). University of Michigan. https://deepblue.lib.umich.edu/bitstream/handle/2027.42/77608/patchen.pdf?sequence=1

11 Sherif, M. (1988). *The robbers cave experiment: Intergroup conflict and cooperation* [Original publication as *Intergroup conflict and group relations*]. Wesleyan University Press.

12 Sometimes extremism can develop without any competition, as a result of isolation where the "normal" pattern of through and behavior is not apparent, and there are no social influences to tamper extreme behaviors. For example, Isaac Newton's isolated lifestyle (in part due to his likely autism, and in part due to the Black Death epidemic that raged through the region and led him to quarantine) allowed him to pursue his scientific interests with extreme dedication and resulted in him developing Calculus and formulating fundamental laws of Physics, among other achievements.

13 Hendrickse, J., Arpan, L. M., Clayton, R. B., & Ridgway, J. L. (2017). Instagram and college women's body image: Investigating the roles of appearance-related comparisons and intrasexual competition. *Computers in Human Behavior*, 74, 92–100. https://doi.org/10.1016/j.chb.2017.04.027

14 Sherlock, M., & Wagstaff, D. L. (2019). Exploring the relationship between frequency of Instagram use, exposure to idealized images, and psychological well-being in women. *Psychology of Popular Media Culture*, 8(4), 482–490. https://doi.org/10.1037/ppm0000182

15 Wilksch, S. M., O'Shea, A., Ho, P., Byrne, S., & Wade, T. D. (2019). The relationship between social media use and disordered eating in young adolescents. *International Journal of Eating Disorders*, 53(1), 96–106. https://doi.org/10.1002/eat.23198

16 Bloom, M., & Moskalenko, S. (2021). *Pastels and pedophiles: Inside the mind of QAnon*. Stanford University Press.

17 Moskalenko, S., Burton, B. S., Fernández-Garayzábal González, J., & Bloom, M. M. (2023). Secondhand conspiracy theories: The social, emotional and political tolls on loved ones of QAnon followers. *Democracy and Security*, 19(3), 231–250.

18 Burton, B., & Moskalenko, S. (2023, Summer). Perceptions versus reality of QAnon radicalization: A comparative study. *Journal for Deradicalization*, 35, 174–207.

19 Jia, K. M., Hanage, W. P., Lipsitch, M., Johnson, A. G., Amin, A. B., Ali, A. R., Scobie, H. M., & Swerdlow, D. L. (2023). Estimated preventable COVID-19-associated deaths due to non-vaccination in the United States. *European Journal of Epidemiology*, 38(11), 1125–1128. https://doi.org/10.1007/s10654-023-01006-3

20 Bradley, S. (2024, January 16). How much money Instagram influencers make. *Business Insider*. https://www.businessinsider.com/how-do-instagram-influencers-make-money

21 Min, S. (2019, November 8). 86% of young Americans want to become a social media influencer. *CBS News*. https://www.cbsnews.com/news/social-media-influencers-86-of-young-americans-want-to-become-one/

22 Liu, J. (2023, September 20). More than half of Gen Zers think they "can easily make a career in influencing," says branding expert. CNBC. https://www.cnbc.com/2023/09/20/more-than-half-of-gen-zers-think-they-can-easily-make-a-career-in-influencing.html#:~:text=Some%2053%25%20of%20Gen%20Zers,pay%20to%20become%20an%20influencer.

23 Jennings, R. (2022, August 31). So your kid wants to be an influencer. Vox. https://www.vox.com/the-goods/2022/8/31/23328677/kid-influencer-ryans-world-ellie-zeiler

24 Catherall, S. (2021, January 30). How social media influencers inspire young people to starve themselves. Stuff. https://www.stuff.co.nz/life-style/well-good/teach-me/300216275/how-social-media-influencers-inspire-young-people-to-starve-themselves

25 Santiago, M. (2023, May 24). We're all shopping addicts now. The Cut. https://www.thecut.com/2023/05/shopping-addiction-online-consumption.html

26 Biaudet, S. (2017). Influencer marketing as a marketing tool: The process of creating an influencer marketing campaign on Instagram. Theseus. https://urn.fi/URN:NBN:fi:amk-2017100615814

27 Glaser, E. (2021, May 17). Many Americans struggle with debt. Social media doesn't help. Vox. https://www.vox.com/the-goods/22436051/social-media-credit-card-debt-instagram-tiktok

28 Furlong, A. (2021, December 7). Going viral? how covid-19 turbocharged snake oil and quackery. Politico. https://www.politico.eu/article/pandemic-misinformation-coronavirus-chronic-diseases-diabetes-cancer-infodemic/

29 Furlong, A. (2021, December 7). Going viral? how covid-19 turbocharged snake oil and quackery. Politico. https://www.politico.eu/article/pandemic-misinformation-coronavirus-chronic-diseases-diabetes-cancer-infodemic/

30 Campillo, J. T., & Faillie, J. L. (2022). Adverse drug reactions associated with ivermectin use for COVID-19 reported in the world health organization's pharmacovigilance database. Therapie, 77(6), 747–749. https://doi.org/10.1016/j.therap.2022.03.002

31 Seiger, T. (2021, September 27). Coronavirus: 2 deaths linked to Ivermectin in New Mexico, officials say. KIRO 7 News Seattle. https://www.kiro7.com/news/trending/coronavirus-2-deaths-linked-ivermectin-new-mexico-officials-say/5SZ55BRSFRDGTLJZ7ODKGZP6XI/

32 Hummel, K. (2020, December 28). The Christchurch attacks: Livestream terror in the viral video age. Combating Terrorism Center at West Point. https://ctc.westpoint.edu/christchurch-attacks-livestream-terror-viral-video-age/

33 Mackintosh, E., & Mezzofiore, G. (2019, October 10). How the extreme-right gamified terror. CNN. https://www.cnn.com/2019/10/10/europe/germany-synagogue-attack-extremism-gamified-grmintl/index.html

34 BBC. (2018, April 25). Elliot Rodger: How misogynist killer became "incel hero." BBC News. https://www.bbc.com/news/world-us-canada-43892189

35 Cecco, L. (2019, September 27). Toronto van attack suspect says he was "radicalized" online by "incels." The Guardian. https://www.theguardian.com/world/2019/sep/27/alek-minassian-toronto-van-attack-interview-incels

36 Moskalenko, S., González, J. F. G., Kates, N., & Morton, J. (2022). Incel ideology, radicalization and mental health: A survey study. The Journal of Intelligence, Conflict, and Warfare, 4(3), 1–29.

37 Moskalenko, S., Kates, N., González, J. F. G., & Bloom, M. (2022). Predictors of radical intentions among incels: A survey of 54 self-identified incels. Journal of Online Trust and Safety, 1(3).

5

NARRATIVES OF EXTREMISM

Extremism is a largely human phenomenon. For the most part, non-human animals give up on things that are too hard instead of per-severating; they tend to run away from things that are too scary, and they avoid things that can cause them harm. This doesn't make them any less successful among the species—in fact it makes them more evolutionarily fit. Julia Keller, a Pulitzer-winning journalist made a compelling case that it might be a winning approach for humans, too, in her aptly titled book, *Quitting: A Life Strategy* (2023). To "know when to fold "em, know when to walk away and know when to run," as the song goes, can save one a lot of trouble.

As Keller put it,

> human beings tend to adhere to the Gospel of Grit—while other creatures on this magnificently diverse earth of ours follow a dif-ferent strategy. Their lives are marked by purposeful halts, fortui-tous side steps, canny retreats, nick-of-time recalculations, wily workarounds, and deliberate do-overs, not to mention loops, pivots, and complete reversals. Other animals, that is, quit on a regular basis. And they don't obsess about it, either.[1]

A honeybee encountering a threat to the colony can sting an intruder, but that sting is fatal to the bee, and a bee will often give

DOI: 10.4324/9781003472476-5

up on the mission to protect the colony at the cost of its own life if the threat is not lethal enough or the colony is not thriving and cannot afford to lose its member. A finch will try to remove seed from its sheath, but only for a little while; if the sheath fails to break, the finch will move on to other food sources rather than keep hammering it with its beak, losing energy and time that could be spent more productively.

In an interview with a notable evolutionary biologist, professor emeritus at the University of Chicago, Jerry Coyne, Keller asked what it is that leads humans to stick it out, to persevere, to get going when the going gets tough—where other animals would have long quit and moved on. Coyne emphasized that humans, just like other animals, have evolved to maximize their survival and reproductive benefits.

> Human behavior has been molded to help us obtain a favorable outcome… We go for what works. We're biased toward results. Yet somewhere between the impulse to follow what strikes us as the most promising path—which means quitting an unpromising path—and the simple act of giving up, something often gets in the way. And that's the mystery that intrigues me: When quitting is the right thing to do, why don't we always do it?[2]

We believe the answer to this question, the solution to the mystery of what comes between the impulse to act and the act of giving up an unpromising path is the uniquely human ability: to tell tales, to spin stories, to create narratives. Narratives tell us of past and future, of what makes a good person or a noble action, of values, beliefs, and aspirations; they can obscure the biological reality of the present moment, make us forget our hunger, thirst, fatigue, and physical pain while we pursue a goal that extends beyond the here and now. Animals can have complex emotions, they can have ideas of fairness and justice, they can solve engineering problems and communicate with one another—but they do not have narratives the way humans do.

Narratives create a shared reality[3] complete with norms, ideals, prohibitions, and prescriptions. These allow us to unite our forces and divide our responsibilities, work in concert, and transcend individual limitations. Narratives have built human civilization, enabled the construction of cities, roads, palaces, and planes—all of which require coordination, planning, and, most relevant to us, the determined pursuit of goals despite the costs and sacrifices they entail.

The biblical story from the Book of Genesis says there was a time when people all "had one language and the same words."[4] They decided to build a city and a great tower that would reach to the Heavens—quite an extreme goal. Learning of this, God became concerned. "And the Lord said, 'Look, they are one people, and they have all one language, and this is only the beginning of what they will do; nothing that they propose to do will now be impossible for them.[7] Come, let us go down and confuse their language there, so that they will not understand one another's speech.'"[8] The story of the Tower of Babel, a human ambition to rise above their humanity to the heights of the Divine that was thwarted by God, hints at the importance of language in human pursuits. Sharing a language is what allows the creation of extremist narratives, whether it is about building a tower to the sky to make one equal to God, opposing a government, fighting a war, or rebuilding in its aftermath.

Sometimes it takes a charismatic leader to create and broadcast a narrative that inspires many followers to extreme actions. Some of Jesus' followers were tortured and killed for the narrative they believed, persevering in their faith despite the mounting and deadly costs. Other followers of Jesus waged Crusades against non-believers, burning and pillaging their cities and forcing them to subscribe to the narrative, extracting extreme costs from others in the name of the narrative they believed. Still others tortured and burned at the stake those who did not fit within the Christian Church's narrative they espoused. These extreme actions have shaped Western civilization, defining the world as we know it today—for a narrative.

Charismatic leaders of modern times, too, can convince millions to embrace their narrative and, once they do, to engage in extreme actions for it. Martin Luther King's speech, "I have a dream," written in a prison cell, has stirred countless others to fight for civil liberties for African Americans by participating in protests that they knew were bound to result in brutal police crackdowns, deaths, injuries, and imprisonment. Moved by Mahatma Gandhi's narrative of an India free of the British Empire's oppression, his followers marched unarmed toward British soldiers beating them on the head with batons, and stood up against British rifles firing on them.[5] A bee would stay away. A finch would give up on a fight that could result in its injury or death. But for humans, a powerful narrative delivered by a charismatic leader can render their own wellbeing less important than the imagined rewards: an afterlife, freedom and justice, a postcolonial homeland, the symbolic immortality of having one's name engraved forever in one's group's collective memory. Humans can give up everything—for a story.

Sometimes narratives that spur political extremism are works of literary fiction. *Uncle Tom's Cabin*, a novel about a long-suffering African American slave, was said to inspire many to join the cause of abolition, helping to lay the groundwork for the Civil War[6] fought over the refusal of Southern states to abolish slavery. It became the second best-selling book in the 19th century USA (Bible was number one),[7] influencing such prominent political figures as Frederick Douglass and a Union General and politician James Baird Weaver.[8] On the other side of the world, in the 19th century Russian Empire, a pro-democracy student movement was similarly inspired by *What's to Be Done*, a novel written by a political prisoner from his prison cell and calling on readers to engage in extreme behaviors in the service of their democratic ideals, from becoming vegetarians and sleeping on a bed of nails to practicing open relationships (as opposed to the oppression of monogamy). Vladimir Lenin, the leader of the Russian Bolshevik revolution, claimed that the book "thoroughly plowed" him, that he read it five times in one summer, and for a while emulated the main character's advice by eating little, sleeping only 4 hours a night, lifting weights, and denying himself romantic relationships.[9] A generation of Russian extremists drew inspiration from the novel, and fueled their radicalization by its ideas.

There is something uniquely powerful about a well-crafted narrative: it can shift our perspective and move our emotions so much that we feel we can't just sit there, that we must do something—even if the doing carries extreme costs. And when a compelling narrative is shared by many, it gains an additional power: to make the costly action seem normative rather than aberrant, reducing the psychological barriers to engaging in it. Especially among young people, when friends endorse an extreme action, whether it is eating laundry detergent pods[10] or engaging in bullying or violence against others or against self[11] social contagion carried by shared narratives is a powerful vehicle for extremism.[12]

To be sure, a narrative alone is unlikely to make someone extremist. Try reading *What's to Be Done* or *Uncle Tom's Cabin* today, and you will likely find them naive if not manipulative, certainly not the kind of reading that would move you to take up political struggle at high personal costs. Even in their day, as much influence as these books wielded over one side of the issue, they did not inspire people on the other side: Russian monarchists did not spend sleepless nights poring over their well-worn copies of *What's to Be Done*, and pro-slavery Southerners in the USA detested and ridiculed *Uncle Tom's Cabin*.[13] Neither was it the literary genius behind the novels that was responsible for their influence. A literary critic said about *Uncle Tom's Cabin*,

> Nothing attributable to Mrs. Stowe or her handiwork can account for the novel's enormous vogue; its author's resources as a purveyor of Sunday-school fiction were not remarkable. She had at most a ready command of broadly conceived melodrama, humor, and pathos, and of these popular sentiments she compounded her book.[14]

Likewise, *Encyclopedia Britannica* deemed *What's to Be Done* "Appallingly bad from a literary point of view."[15] So what is the secret behind these narratives' power to move people to extremes?

One answer comes from the study of a more recent narrative, that of QAnon conspiracy theories.[16] Participants in the study were selected if they had never heard the QAnon narrative about a Satan-worshipping cabal of pedophiles who have taken over the US government and the media and who kidnap, torture, and sexually abuse children to harvest the brutalized children's blood for *adrenochrome*, a substance that is supposed to give "special powers" to those who consume it. Half the participants read a brief version of this narrative (similar to the description above), and were asked how much they believed this narrative. They then answered questions about what kinds of behaviors they would engage in to advance or protect a group that is important to them, such as their religious group, ethnic group, national group, etc. The other half of the participants answered questions about behavioral intentions first, then read the conspiratorial narrative and answered how much they believed it. Those who read the narrative first, as compared to those who answered questions about behavioral intentions first, expressed more extreme behavioral intentions to support their group, including intentions to participate in violent riots, and to attack police and security forces if they were mistreating members of the participant's group. But this was ONLY true for participants who expressed any belief in the narrative in the first place. Those who, when asked how much they believed the story about the cabal, answered "Not at all" were not moved to extreme action. In other words, how much a new narrative can increase someone's extremism depends on how much they believe its message.

And what determines that? Possibly something about the personality, inborn tendencies to respond to situations in particular kinds of ways, plays a role. There is, as we mentioned earlier, mounting evidence for an "extremist personality," the kind of impetuous person who is ready to "go for broke" and develop a passion for a topic to the exclusion of all else. Evidence gathered by Dr Ewa Szumowska of the Jagiellonian University in Poland shows also that people who have an extreme personality can become extremists in a variety of different domains in which they develop an interest. Dr Szumowska's work attests that such persons are as likely to engage in extreme sports as in extreme dieting, and in extreme sexual practices.[17]

No less important, however, are certain individual Needs and social Networks that can combine with the right Narrative to foster the development of extremist ideas or behaviors. An individual who has a high *Need for significance*, a desire to achieve recognition, respect and admiration, may see a narrative of suffering children at the hands of evil monsters as a chance to gain significance: becoming a hero, adopting an extremist stance to fight the cabal and save the children. And if this kind of Narrative of innocents' suffering becomes widely accepted in one's community or circle, if many in one's Network subscribe to its message and endorse extremist actions to address the injustice, this makes the likelihood of extremist action inspired by the narrative even more likely. Endorsement of a narrative by people one respects—charismatic leaders, friends, and others in one's inner circle—validates it and makes it more believable. It is not only that one trusts the judgments and opinions of these people, but one also wishes to agree with and be accepted by them; all this increases the believability of the narrative they support, and turns it into a shared reality in group members' eyes. The 3N model[18] predicts that political radicalization is the result of Needs, Networks, and Narratives aligning in such a way.

NARRATIVES ARE US

But narratives don't only coordinate the actions of many. They also direct actions of individuals, every one of us. Think back to the time you felt the odds were against you, and you thought of giving up—but did not. What was going through your mind just then that made you go on? Was it your mother's voice telling you that you can do it? Or perhaps your father's voice telling you to not be a quitter? Your coach's favorite saying that winners never quit, and quitters never win? Was it your own hard-won ideas and beliefs about what is the right thing to do and how to do it? Or a favorite fictional charac-ter, Frodo from Lord of the Rings or Harry Potter who persevered against seemingly insurmountable odds, serving as your model and inspiration? Human mind is a constantly churning narrative-maker, connecting every dot that comes into its view into a cohesive and consistent story.

In some ways, we *are* the stories we tell ourselves and the world. Oliver Sacks, a famous neurologist, suggested that our individual identities are nothing but a narrative we construct for ourselves and the world.

> We have, each of us, a life-story, an inner narrative—whose continuity, whose sense, is our lives. It might be said that each of us constructs and lives, a "narrative," and that this narrative is us, our identities. If we wish to know about a man, we ask "what is his story—his real, inmost story?"—for each of us is a biography, a story. Each of us is a singular narrative, which is constructed, continually, unconsciously, by, through, and in us—through our perceptions, our feelings, our thoughts, our actions; and, not least, our discourse, our spoken narrations. Biologically, physiologically, we are not so different from each other; historically, as narratives—we are each of us unique.[19]

To illustrate the importance of narrative to identity, Sacks tells of a patient afflicted by a memory disorder that stripped away his ability to recognize not just others, but even himself. This patient became incapable of retaining the personal memories that form one's sense of self. In response to this amnesic condition, the patient crafted a myriad of fantastical tales about his identity and life experiences, filling the void of his identity with a multitude of imagined personas and adventures. Our minds are so adept at creating narratives, so uniquely designed for the task that in the absence of facts they spin them out of fiction.

A sizable body of research in psychology demonstrates that people's memories are often altered: rewritten, as it were. Sometimes this editing of the recollection of the past happens because of events in the present, such as the phrasing of questions that police interrogators ask witnesses about the crime.[20] Other times it is a result selective retention of information at the time of the event—committing to memory only the facts that confirm a pre-existing narrative while neglecting and forgetting those that dispute it[21]—a tendency also known as confirmation bias. We think what we know are hard facts, but instead they are stories.

And, interestingly, not only do we create narratives to make up for missing memories, but we also remember things better if we make up a story about them. Memory buffs use this mnemonic, called descriptive story technique, to memorize things such as lists of unrelated items. Putting unrelated things together into a single story makes them easier to recall.

Our mental narrative-making does not stop even when we go to sleep, because dreams are narratives, too. Sometimes related to the real-world problems we struggle with in wakeful hours, dreams can offer a suggestion, an answer, or a new perspective on what the wakeful storyteller is too shy or too polite to suggest. As John Gottschall said in his book, The storytelling animal, "We are, as a species, addicted to story, Even when the body goes to sleep, the mind stays up all night, telling itself stories" (p. xiv).[22]

In fact, it is very hard to stop the mind from spinning stories. Those who learn to meditate or practice mindfulness, discover just how difficult it is to turn off the narrative (or narratives) running through one's head—even in the absence of any outside input. It takes years of consistent practice to quiet down the internal storyteller, and even then it springs up now and then, reminding the self about the chores that need to be done, rehashing a conversation from the past, or rehearsing an event in the future. This storyteller in our head can be judgmental or kind, approving or scolding, but whatever the tone, it has power over us because it comes from the time when we were little and powerless, just learning about the vast and unknown world.

OUR NARRATIVES ARE SOCIALLY CONSTRUCTED

We are hardly the sole authors of our narratives. The stories we spin about ourselves, our identities, the notions of who we are, and who we want to be are socially constructed. From various significant others—our parents, teachers, leaders, friends—we learn what is desirable and what is abhorrent, what is important and what is trivial. We learn what group we belong to, which of our aspects (intelligence, gender, skin color, body shape) matter to others, and what can be done about it. These notions, concepts, categories, and values that significant others impart to us are the building blocks we put together to construct the meanings we ascribe to ourselves, other people, and events.

From a very early age, children learn about the world outside of their immediate experience through fairy tales: stories that caretakers in their lives selected and told them, thus placing the seal of approval of the child's most important social Network on these particular Narratives ("I am your parent and I approve this message"). Fairy tales serve an important role in early socialization: they indoctrinate children into the moral norms of their society, teaching them about right and wrong, good and bad by colorful and memorable examples. By identifying with the main character of a fairy tale, the child can vicariously experience the triumph of their happy ending, which comes from the character's culturally approved traits, such as cleverness, hard work, or loyalty. In a way, the child goes on a virtual significance quest, fulfilling their Need to feel important, respected and admired through their connection with the fairy tale's character who achieves all these things. In this process of listening to fairy tales, identifying with their characters, and partaking of the characters' significance, the child internalizes the fairy tales' moral lessons. The storyteller voice inside an adult's head that says, "keep going, you can do it" when the going gets tough, the voice that says "well done" when sacrifices pay off—that voice may have started out by saying, "Once upon a time, in a land far, far away…" Significance

Needs of adulthood rely on lessons of childhood Narratives for how to live "happily ever after" basking in the approval of one's Network.

EXTREMISM'S UNIQUE APPEAL

Children are not a very patient bunch, but fairy tales grab hold of their attention, because they speak not of ordinary things, everyday chores and routine—but of heroes and villains, superpowers and feats of extraordinary courage, or kindness, or greed, or cruelty. In short, fairy tales spin stories of extremism. Cinderella was forbidden by her stepmother to go to the ball—but instead of going along to get along, she tried and tried, worked hard and persevered until she got what she wanted despite the odds. Hansel and Gretel were taken to the forest by their father and left there to die, but Hansel intervened again and again, rising up to ever more difficult challenges through his wit and determination, until finally bringing himself and his sister home, and with treasures to support the family, too, so there would be no more attempts to exile the children. Children's fairy tales, in short, glorify extremism, praise persevering against the odds and obstacles, reward single-minded dedication to a goal, and promise rewards for such actions.

And not just children's fairy tales. Blockbuster movies and best-selling novels rarely talk of "regular people who never did anything extraordinary." Instead, they present heroes and super-heroes, hobbits whose dedication to save the world puts men to shame, near-sighted orphaned boys who defeat the greatest evil wizards of all times, lovers who would rather die than be apart, the poor who make millions, and millionaires who squander their riches away. Stories of extremism grab hold of adults' attention just as much as fairy tales mesmerize children. And just as children, we can't help but identify with the main character, imagine ourselves with those extraordinary powers, that kind of love, that kind of wealth. We wish we were the main character in a story like that. We wish we were extreme like that.

The extremist narrative makes salient something of supreme importance, usually a universal human need (for survival, for dignity, for honor, for love) whose fulfillment spells bliss, and unfulfillment disaster. It affirms that in the circumstances given, the only way to fulfill the need is through sacrifice and self-denial. Thus, in deciding to carry out an extreme act one faces a tough predicament: the need to risk losing or actually giving up something of value to gain or protect something of an even greater value. That is why extremism is so rare; most people are unable or unwilling to pay the price that extremism demands. And that is also why extremism, when it occurs, is often short-lived. The denied needs, sacrificed on an altar of the prioritized concern, soon reassert their existential importance; the motivational, extremism-spawning imbalance is difficult to sustain, and ultimately moderation prevails. That is also why extremist narratives are so awe-inspiring, why their protagonists become our admired heroes, larger-than-life demigods, and inspirational models.

It's not that there are no narratives of moderation, of the everyday, nothing special, business as usual—it's just that they don't stand a chance in the marketplace of ideas, with attention spans growing ever shorter, and expectations rising ever higher. The stories that stand out in this crowded field tend to be stories of extremism; they end up being the ones to shape our ideas of how to be and what to hope for. They stick in our heads as an internal storyteller who won't leave us in peace day or night, spinning our own life into a story that is measured against an extreme standard. Lucky for birds and bees to not have that kind of pressure.

The following chapter will explore the ill effects this pressure can have on mental health. You might not be surprised that talk therapy, which helps the patient to give voice to their internal storyteller, as well as to alter the narrative that causes their suffering, can be an effective remedy for mental health issues.

Sometimes, no therapist is needed to identify the problematic extremist narrative, and to change it. Especially if the person is one of the most famous storytellers of our time. Steven Spielberg, a multiple Oscars-winning movie director recounted in his memoir one such instance. He was filming *Close Encounters of the Third Kind*, a project that followed his blockbuster success, *Jaws*. The production was over budget and behind schedule, but more troublingly for Spielberg was the nagging narrative in his head that the movie must top the success of *Jaws*, an unlikely feat given that Jaws beat record after record as the highest-grossing film, overtaking box office success of *The Godfather*, and becoming the highest-earning film of all times. Spielberg described crumbling under the pressure of his own making, until one day he climbed on top of the dirigible hangar where the filming was taking place to have a breath of fresh air. Standing on top of the 8-story scaffolding structure, Spielberg said, "looking down at this 400 × 200-foot concept…I laughed." The extremist narrative in his head, the one that told him he should have two blockbusters in a row, suddenly seemed ridiculous. Nobody expects one mega-hit, let alone two, he realized. After that change in perspective, Spielberg changed his internal narrative, the script inside his head. Instead of telling himself he must top the success of his previous hit, he told himself he should feel the confidence of his competence, proven by the success of his previous hit. After this, Spielberg climbed back down the scaffolding structure and finished filming *Close Encounters*. It became another critical and commercial success, grossing $306.9 million worldwide.[23]

We cannot change the personality we are born in, or the network which raises us; we cannot change the past, and often we can't change the present. However, the story in our head, should we be lucky enough to identify it the way Steven Spielberg did, is within our control. The same set of mental building blocks can be rearranged to construct different narrative edifices. When we find ourselves in the grip of a destructive extremist narrative, we can change it.

IN SUMMARY

The reason zebras don't have extremists (a spin on Robert Sapolsky's bestselling book, *Why zebras don't have ulcers*) is because young zebra never hear stories about zebra extremists that they would want to emulate: Prometheus, Prophet Mohammed, Jesus, Honest Abe, Johnny Appleseed, Lenin, or Mao. The reason people sometimes become extreme is that they follow in the footsteps of fictional or fictionalized heroes in a desperate quest to matter and have significance. With globalization, 24-hour news cycle, the social media and smart mobile devices at everyone's fingertips, the stories priming extremism are more abundant than ever. QAnon's narratives of evil lizard people and child snatchers lurking in the shadows, for example, fall neatly into the grooves of early fairytales, and the idea of "Making America Great Again" or "Making Russia Great Again" fit like a glove the outlines of significance quests formed in early childhood and re-activated by the barrage of news and narratives.

NOTES

1   Keller, J. (2023, April 19). Quitting is a wildly underrated life strategy. Here's why. *Big Think*. https://bigthink.com/neuropsych/neuroscience-of-quitting/

2   Keller, J. (2023, April 19). Quitting is a wildly underrated life strategy. Here's why. *Big Think*. https://bigthink.com/neuropsych/neuroscience-of-quitting/

3   Higgins, T. E. (2019). *Shared reality: What makes us strong and tears us apart*. Oxford University Press.

4   The Bible. (1989). *The new revised standard version*. https://biblia.com/bible/nrsv/genesis/11/1-9

5   Moskalenko, S., & McCauley, C. (2018). *The marvel of martyrdom: The power of self-sacrifice in a selfish world*. Oxford University Press.

6   Painter, N. I. (2000). Honest abe and uncle tom. *Canadian Review of American Studies, 30*(3), 245–272. doi:10.3138/CRAS-s030-03–01.

7   DiMaggio, K. (2014). Uncle Tom's cabin: Global best seller, anti-slave narrative, imperialist agenda. *Global Studies Journal, 7*(1), 15–23. doi:10.18848/1835-4432/CGP/46892.

8   Arnett, A. M. (1920, March). Review of James Baird Weaver by Fred Emory Haynes. *Political Science Quarterly, 35*(1), 154–157. doi:10.2307/2141508.

9   McCauley, C. R., & Moskalenko, S. (2017). *Friction: How conflict radicalizes them and us*. Oxford University Press.

10 Kriegel, E. R., Lazarevic, B., Athanasian, C. E., & Milanaik, R. L. (2021). TikTok, Tide Pods and Tiger King: Health implications of trends taking over

pediatric populations. *Current Opinion in Pediatrics*, 33(1), 170–177. https://doi.org/10.1097/MOP.0000000000000989

11 Martínez, V., Jiménez-Molina, Á., & Gerber, M. M. (2023). Social contagion, violence, and suicide among adolescents. *Current Opinion in Psychiatry*, 36(3), 237–242. https://doi.org/10.1097/YCO.0000000000000858

12 Forsyth, M., & Gibbs, P. (2020). Contagion of violence: The role of narratives, worldviews, mechanisms of transmission and contagion entrepreneurs. *International Journal for Crime, Justice and Social Democracy*, 9(2), 37–59. 10.5204/ijcjsd.v9i2.1217.

13 PBS. (2007). *Slave narratives and Uncle Tom's cabin*. Africans in America. Retrieved February 16, 2007, from https://www.pbs.org/wgbh/aia/part4/4p2956.html

14 Tompkins, J. (1985). Sentimental power: Uncle Tom's cabin and the politics of literary history. In J. Tompkins (Ed.), *Sensational designs: The cultural work of American fiction, 1790–1860* (p. 126). Oxford University Press.

15 *Russian literature*. Academic Dictionaries and Encyclopedias. (n.d.). https://universalium.en academic.com/286039/Russian_literature

16 Moskalenko, S., Pavlovic, T., & Romanova, E. (2024). Mere exposure to conspiracy theories: Effects on radical intentions among believers and nonbelievers. *Behavioral Sciences of Terrorism and Political Aggression*, 1–25. https://www.tandfonline.com/doi/abs/10.1080/19434472.2024.2396282.

17 Szumowska, E., Molinario, E., Jasko, K., HUdiyana, J., Firdiani, N. F., Penrod, J., & Kruglanski, A. W. (2024). *The extreme personality: Individual differences in proneness to motivational imbalance*. Unpublished manuscript. University of Maryland.

18 Kruglanski, A. W., Molinario, E., Ellenberg, M., & Di Cicco, G. (2022). Terrorism and conspiracy theories: A view from the 3N model of radicalization. *Current Opinion in Psychology*, 47, Article 101396. https://doi.org/10.1016/j.copsyc.2022.101396

19 Sacks, O. (2011). *The man who mistook his wife for a hat: And other clinical tales* (p. 114). Brilliance Audio.

20 Gerrie, M. P., Garry, M., & Loftus, E. F. (2005). False memories. *Psychology and Law: An Empirical Perspective*, 1, 222–253.

21 Oswald, M. E., & Grosjean, S. (2004). Confirmation bias. In *Cognitive illusions: A handbook on fallacies and biases in thinking, judgement and memory* (Vol. 79, p. 83). Psychology Press. https://doi.org/10.13140/2.1.2068.0641

22 Gottschall, J. (2012). *The storytelling animal: How stories make us human*. Houghton Mifflin Harcourt.

23 Oppenheimer, B. (2024, January 7). A change in perspective is worth 80 IQ points. *Six and 6 on Sunday*. https://billyoppenheimer.com/january-7-2024/

6

MENTAL HEALTH AND EXTREMISM

In the previous chapter, we asserted that extremism is a largely human phenomenon, driven to a great degree by narratives only humans can create. Yet, animals can also exhibit extremism.

Consider for example a cat named Misha. Misha was the last addition to a household that already had a dog and two other cats. One of the other cats, Rocco, was rather mean to everyone, but poor Misha got the worst of his bullying. Rocco chased Misha away from the food bowl, spooked him when he tried to use the litter box, and ambushed Misha from any and every height and corner. Shortly after joining the household, Misha developed an obsession: he started biting his own fur off everywhere he could reach. He spent every waking moment doing it, until only his head had remaining fur, and the rest of him was bold and gray, covered with scabs—the results of particularly vigorous fur extermination. Misha did not stop the war on fur after becoming bold; now he spent all his time licking himself in search of new growth, and, at the first signs of it biting into it with fervor. He looked and acted miserable. However, playing with him, petting him, or any other attempts to distract him from his obsession was futile: Misha evaded them, sometimes with annoyance, to focus on his one goal in life, which was to eradicate his fur.

A veterinarian examined Misha and deemed him physically healthy. In fact, Misha embodied an animal model of extremism, when one goal overshadows all others, sometimes to the detriment

DOI: 10.4324/9781003472476-6

of the individual pursuing it. We will never know what need drew Misha to the extreme behavior he displayed. Was it a way to distract himself from Rocco's bullying? Or perhaps he internalized Rocco's despise of him, and "identified with the aggressor" as Dr Freud might have opined. Be it as it may, Misha's behavior properly qualifies as extremism both because of its focused, single-minded nature, carried out to the exclusion of nearly all else, and because of its self-denying nature, depriving the poor cat of an invaluable asset meant to keep him warm and protected from the elements.

If Misha's symptoms (self-inflicted, persistent hair pulling that results in bold spots) were observed in a person, that person would likely receive a psychiatric diagnosis of trichotillomania. Trichotillomania is a mental health disorder that falls within the category of impulse-control disorders. People afflicted with it have a persistent and irresistible urge to pull out the hair on their head, their eyebrows, and eyelashes, and sometimes to bite or chew on the pulled hair. It's an embarrassing condition whose obvious signs (bold patches) create new reasons for anxiety about being judged, a vicious cycle. The patient's work and social life suffer as a result of their compulsive behavior, which, along with the attempts to hide the bold spots, can in severe cases take over one's life. Trichotillomania is a mental health disorder that fits the model of extremism.

For Misha, years of suffering from Rocco's bullying ended when Rocco passed away from old age. With the bullying over, so was Misha's relentless behavior. In only a few months, he went from a dreadful-looking obsessive creature to a handsome and friendly tubby.

Social exclusion and bullying are painful experiences. Neuroscience research shows that human brain processes social rejection in the same brain regions where physical pain is detected and processed (dorsal anterior cingulate cortex (dACC) and anterior insula (AI)).[1] Being rejected and ostracized is painful, and being bullied can result in psychological trauma.

Misha the cat was ultimately able to bounce back from the experience of being ostracized and bullied—but for humans it's not always easy. As the saying goes, you can take a person out of a traumatic situation, but you can't always take the traumatic situation out of a person. Chapter 5 describes how people differ from animals in our ability to create narratives that transcend time and space. Getting out of a traumatic situation does not necessarily stop the internal story-teller from spinning a narrative about it. Stories created during or about a painful time can integrate the trauma into the self-concept, identity, self-worth, and meanings attached to the present and the future. Long after the bullying is over, the narratives may continue to reverberate inside the victim's head, telling them they deserve bad things to happen to them, that nobody cares about them, or that they need to punish themselves or to punish others for the pain they are feeling.

IMBALANCE, PSYCHOPATHOLOGY, AND EXTREMISM

This kind of negative self-talk is likely to exacerbate the trauma of the past and extend it into the present. Trying to silence the painful internal narrative, individuals might engage in a variety of extreme behaviors, some of which fall within the definitions of mental health disorders. Thus, people who have experienced bullying as children, and therefore experienced profound losses to their sense of significance and mattering, are more likely to develop substance abuse issues[2] as well as other mental health problems including anxiety and depression.[3] They are also more likely to engage in self-harming behaviors.[4]

Many mental health disorders, whether they begin as a response to external events, as was the case for Misha, or are endemic (due to internal causes, like genetics)—take on a form of extremism. Like other extremists, people afflicted with such conditions are inordinately focused on a particular issue or goal and neglect other aspects of their lives. People with anxiety disorders, such as obsessive-compulsive disorder (OCD), may spend most of their time worrying (obsessing) over some possible harm they may suffer or inflict on others. They also spend time in ritualistic and repetitive behaviors (compulsions) meant to reduce the imagined harm, such as washing hands, checking over and over whether some appliance is turned off or whether the door is locked, etc. The obsessions and compulsions create a severe motivational imbalance, and take over one's mental horizon, leaving little space for anything else. The person suffering from the disorder becomes consumed with thoughts and behaviors related to the disorder, at great costs to their social and professional life. Depending on the severity, an anxiety disorder may literally hold the person hostage, as is the case of people suffering from severe ago-raphobia (fear of open spaces), who never leave their own homes, imprisoned by an overriding fear of the outdoors.

Likewise, depression is often characterized by ruminative thoughts, mostly about one's low self-worth or insignificance. People suffer-ing from depression tend to rehash over and over a negative belief (i.e. "I am just no good;" "Nobody will ever love me"), or relive a negative memory. Depression makes people feel tired and listless, it detracts from their sleep quality, it affects their appetite and sex drive. In other words, depression can take over one's entire life. In severe cases the person suffering from depression cannot get out of bed, cannot take a shower, cannot go to work or cook a meal for them-selves. Sometimes, depression can lead to suicide. Like other mood disorders, depression is a case of extremism in which one's exagger-ated preoccupation with one's sense of insignificance drowns out all else, with the person's social connections, work, and hobbies fad-ing as depression saps most of the individual's mental and physi-cal energies.

The progression to extremism is perhaps especially clear in sub-stance abuse disorders. Usually, an individual starts by being able to moderate their intake of the drug, be it alcohol or another sub-stance. However, after some time and with continued and increasing use, all other concerns—family, work, friends, hobbies, and leisure activities—fall by the wayside. More and more resources, money, energy, and time are directed toward substance use. This progression can result in a loss of one's job, and family, one's friends and social connections. The losses exacerbate substance use, until the person finds themselves entirely preoccupied and consumed with only one desire, one goal: to get the next "hit," no matter the cost or the consequences. Substance abuse can lead users to prostitute themselves, to sell or prostitute their own children, to participate in crimes like theft, burglary, and robbery, even to murder—all in the service of their overriding goal.

Mental health disorders that take on a form of extremism are most harmful to the person who suffers from them. In some cases, however, mental health disorders can result in the kind of extremism that is harmful to others more than to the extremist. Often such disorders can result from a history of bullying and abuse to which the individual was exposed in their childhood.

THE CASE OF JC

Because both authors of this book work in the area of psychology of terrorism and political violence, we occasionally come in contact with individuals who have engaged in such kinds of violent extremism. This is how we both got to know JC (not his real name). JC was well known in the counter-terrorism professional community as a former—someone who at one time was a terrorist or violent extremist, but who ended up working for the "other side"—assisting researchers, security services, and counter-terrorism professionals in their professional efforts. By the time we met JC, he was running his own non-profit company, consulting a number of government agencies and non-profits, and making regular appearances in the media. His story was remarkable.

A White American, JC became enamored with radical Islam. He converted, became fluent in Arabic, married a Muslim woman. A bright man, JC saw an opportunity in the online space that was beginning to grow at that time. He seized it by creating a website to bring radical jihad to English-speaking internet users. It became the most effective English-language website for jihadi propaganda. The Boston Marathon bombers, evidently, got the instructions for making pressure cooker bombs from his website. Eventually, JC was arrested, charged, and sentenced for terrorism-related activity. But soon he chose to cooperate with the authorities, and was released after serving only a fraction of his sentence, becoming an effective part of the intelligence and research community focused on countering and preventing violent extremism.

In person, JC was intelligent, well read, and charming. He was an effective speaker, a popular guest on many podcasts, radio shows and television programs. How did he become an extremist, such a gifted guy?

JC grew up in a rural farmhouse, an eldest child of a stay-at-home mother who became severely abusive toward him: emotionally, verbally, physically, and sexually. The mother was abusive toward one other sibling, but JC got the worst of it, sometimes intentionally drawing the mother's ire away from this younger kin. In the rural area where they lived, nobody could hear the screams coming from the house. Nobody came to rescue the children. At one point, when he was already in high school, JC mustered the courage to complain about the abuse to the school counselor. Instead of alerting the authorities, the counselor called the mother, who convincingly denied wrongdoing. Back at home, JC's attempt to get help resulted instead in an especially brutal and prolonged outburst of abuse.

To escape the oppressive environment, at age 15, JC ran away from home to live on the streets of New York City. This resulted in new trauma: physical, emotional, and sexual. He began using drugs, which led to arrests and imprisonments. It was in prison that JC came across *The Autobiography of Malcolm X*. The endorsement of violence especially resonated with him. So did the ideas of Islam. JC converted, symbolically washing away his troubled past, taking on a new Muslim name to mark the beginning of a new life. But he did not become an average Muslim convert. He became an extremist. The news reports of Al Qaeda's 9/11 attacks against the USA brought him joy: someone was punishing the country that didn't care at all about him, that caused him nothing but pain.

The kind of abuse JC suffered at the hands of the person who was supposed to love him the most, the indifference of people in his childhood to his misery, the dangers and bullying he experienced on the uncaring streets of a big city produced suffering that is difficult to fathom by those of us who are more fortunate. Ostracism and bullying are always painful, but perhaps especially so when foisted by one's own mother.

JC's transition to violent political extremism was preceded by his engagement in other kinds of extremisms. First, he developed substance abuse issues; then he became involved in crime, dealing drugs on a large scale. Only after that did JC progress to violent extremism. As he said, every system has failed him. His own family; the school; the justice system—nobody took the time to help him address the problems he faced. He had ample reasons for feeling angry.

At the time the authors met JC, it seemed as though he has left extremism behind, building a business and a life as a respected professional, a father, and a member of the professional community. However, in moments of candor, this mask of normalcy slipped. He sobbed uncontrollably, and said out loud the kinds of things that made clear that the narrative of his troubled past was still very much with him. "I always F*** things up," he said, "I am just a circus monkey," referencing his work as a former.

In close encounters with JC, other symptoms came through: loud noises and sudden gestures startled him. Occasionally, he grew still and unresponsive in the middle of a dialogue; after some seconds he would shake it off as "just a flashback." JC said he had trouble sleeping, only sleeping 4–5 hours at a time, and suffering from nightmares. He could not recall most of his childhood, whole stretches of time were completely lost to him. All these symptoms were consistent with a diagnosis of post-traumatic stress disorder (PTSD). Unfortunately, JC has never had a psychiatrist of psychologist examine him or perform a diagnostic workup. It is likely that JC's troubled childhood caused him to suffer PTSD, which was further exacerbated and compounded by his life on the streets as a teenager, and his time in the prison system. Without a proper diagnosis or treatment,

JC ended up self-medicating his insomnia, anxiety, shame, guilt for leaving behind his younger abused sibling, and negative self-talk. And his self-medication was with drugs first, then with hate.

Had JC been properly assessed and treated for mental health issues, perhaps he would be able to leave his past behind and capitalize on the many gifts he had. Tragically, this possibility will remain hypothetical. Just weeks before his scheduled psychiatric assessment, JC died by fentanyl overdose, relapsing after years of being drug-free.

After his passing, it became clear that JC continued to be an extremist even as he was working to counter extremism: several women believed they were in an exclusive relationship with him, and more than one was married to him. It must have taken a lot of time, money, and effort to keep up this multi-player ruse. JC seemed to have had tried to soothe his psychic wounds by yet another extremist pursuit.

Mental illness and extremism related to it do not usually result in violence or harm to others. Dutch painter Vincent Van Gogh was severely depressed, a condition for which he was hospitalized several times. He experienced delusions and hallucinations, and in these psychotic episodes neglected his health, forgetting to eat and bathe. He drank heavily and engaged in self-harm (cutting off his own ear). Van Gogh died by suicide at the age of 37, shooting himself in the chest with a revolver.

Although Van Gogh showed signs of mental instability even as a child, it could not have helped that he felt rejected by the public, and alienated from the artistic community, suffering a falling out even with his close friend, Paul Gauguin. The alienation Van Gogh felt pained him tremendously, as we know from his contemporaneous writing. At the same time, it propelled Van Gogh's departure from the styles and tastes of the artists of his time, crystallizing his art into a unique and idiosyncratic style for which we know him. Perhaps the reason we resonate so strongly to *The Starry Night* is that it portrays not just extreme beauty but also extremely painful solitude in the way other artists could not.

ISOLATION AND EXTREMISM

German philosopher, Friedrich Nietzsche, also suffered from severe depression. At age 44, he had a mental breakdown that led to paralysis and dementia.[5] Nietzsche appreciated the relationship between alienation and extremism of his philosophical work. "I go into solitude so as not to drink out of everybody's cistern. When I am among the many I live as the many do, and I do not think I really think."[6] Nietzsche's statement is particularly resonant with what we know about the relation between social deviance and extremism. Most people strive to satisfy all their basic needs; this leads to the formation of social norms that safeguard moderation. Isolation from the crowd liberates from those norms, allowing to pursue one thing to the utmost while neglecting others, ushering in extremism.

Nikola Tesla, a Serbian-American engineer and inventor, after which the famous electric car is named, observed in this connection:

> The mind is sharper and keener in seclusion and uninter-rupted solitude. No big laboratory is needed in which to think. Originality thrives in seclusion free of outside influences beating upon us to cripple the creative mind. Be alone, that is the secret of invention; be alone, that is when ideas are born.[7]

Like JC, Tesla suffered from PTSD. Tesla's mental health disorder stemmed from a traumatic loss of his brother when they were both children. According to Tesla, his late brother had been far more gifted than he, and more beloved by the parents, who became inconsolable after his death. Tesla tried in vain to gain their attention and approval. As an adult, in addition to PTSD, he suffered from other mental health issues, such as obsessions, mood disorders, and impulsive symptoms.[8] It seems that, to attain the kind of innovative thought that marks a genius, to pursue it with extreme dedication and build a body of work around it, social isolation is often a pre-requisite.

DISCRIMINATION AND REJECTION

Or it can be a catalyst. Marie Sklodowska-Curie, whose biography is aptly titled *The Obsessive Genius*,[9] experienced rejection early and often. She seemed to never be good enough for her father, a teacher of mathematics and physics. Even on his deathbed, when learning of his daughter's achievement of isolating radium, all he had to say was, too bad this was a purely theoretical discovery. Marie's first love, for a son of the people for whom she worked as a governess, turned into a tragic loss when his parents forbade him to marry the penniless servant. As a women pursuing science in 18th and early 20th century, Marie Sklodowska-Curie suffered repeated discrimination. She was denied a job at Krakow University because of sexism. The French Academy of Science refused to induct her even after the discoveries of the chemical elements radium and polonium she has made with her husband, Pierre Curie (which won her two Nobel Prizes).[10] When Pierre died, and Marie had an affair with a married colleague, their letters were stolen and printed in newspapers, resulting in public shaming and harassment.

Throughout her life, Curie suffered from severe depression. However, after every rejection she found solace in her work, spending extraordinary amounts of time in the lab among radioactive materials that compromised her health.

MALADAPTIVE EXTREMISM

Psychopathology and extremism are tightly related. In fact, the early attempts to understand why people become violent extremists was to assume that they suffer from some type of mental disorder, narcissism, for example. Since then, research has largely dispelled the idea that violent extremists are necessarily suffering from mental disorders, though some (especially those classified as lone wolf terrorists) might be. It may be well to say that all (or most) individuals who suffer from mental disorders are extremists in the sense of privileging one aspect of their lives over all others, yet not all extremists necessarily suffer from mental disorders. As noted in Chapter 5, some extremists become so due to the powers of the extremist narratives to which they are exposed, and through their social networks that uphold those narratives.

Extremism of any kind is rare (as is psychopathology), and it often goes hand-in-hand with social isolation and rejection. Feeling all alone and ostracized weakens the felt need to consider others' views and compromise one's own to agree with theirs. Consequently, one may feel free to indulge one's imagination to the fullest, and explore ideas and actions far beyond the comfort zone of the mainstream.

It is also possible that for some, rejection and bullying by their peers is not the cause but a result of being extreme. This is especially likely among those who are on the autism spectrum, making them at once more likely to hyper-focus on an idea or interest in an extreme way and to ignore social norms, which can result in ostracism and bullying.

This possibility seems likely among Incels (involuntary celibates) an online community of mostly men who feel disenfranchised in the modern society because they cannot find a female sexual partner. Incels attribute their romantic failings to modern feminism. Several Incels have carried out multi-casualty attacks to avenge their grievances and to inspire extremism among other Incels. In surveys of self-identified Incels, they report extremely high prevalence of mental health issues such as depression and anxiety (rates of about 95%), as well as high prevalence of a history of bullying (86%).[11,12]

Seventy-four percent of Incels also reported that they were on the autism spectrum—a much greater proportion than the <5% of individuals so identified in representative studies of US adults. Too, there was a significant correlation among Incels between a history of bullying and intentions to engage in political violence; but neither depression nor anxiety correlated with radical behavioral intentions. It is possible that being repeatedly bullied (as different and autistic) may lead a person to act out against others and engage in political violence, or turn the upset against oneself and suffer depression and anxiety.

The link between social exclusion and extremism is evident in other populations that engage in extremism. For example, individuals with a history of having been bullied are more likely to become involved in crime.[13] In surveys of American Muslims, feeling socially alienated and persecuted correlated with endorsement of extremist jihadi opinions, such as that bombing of civilians is justified in defense of Islam.[14] In a study of QAnon supporters, greater social alienation correlated with greater belief in QAnon conspiracy theories, as well as a greater support for January 6th insurrectionists, and a greater willingness to engage in political violence.[15]

Bullying and social alienation, however traumatic, do not automatically result in either mental health problems or destructive extremism. In some cases, social rejection can lead one to seek and attain extreme success. This was the case with such star athletes as champion boxer Mike Tyson, legendary hockey player Wayne Gretzky, record-breaking golf player Tiger Woods, and Olympic champion swimmer Michael Phelps. Each has been bullied before becoming successful and famous.[16] Billionaire Elon Musk, who brought the world the electric car Tesla and space exploration program SpaceX, was also bullied as a child.[17] Clearly, extremism that comes on the heels of social rejection and bullying is not necessarily destructive for the society.

Nevertheless, bullying and social alienation are risk factors for extremism. While some people walk away unscathed from social rejection and bullying, for others it can result in an extended psychological trauma that can manifest as personally destructive mental health issues: substance abuse, self-harm, PTSD, depression, and anxiety; as socially destructive extremism: crime, radicalization, and political violence; and in yet other cases as creativity and independence of thought affording the gritty pursuit of one's ideas despite social rejection and misapprehension.

AVOIDING PATHOLOGICAL EXTREMISM

It is impossible to disentangle causality between these three things: alienation, mental health disorders, and extremism. However, if you are an adult living with scars of childhood bullying or with mental health disorders, if you worry that you have extremist tendencies that are ruining your life, there are helpful ways to address these.

1. "Know thyself" said Ancient Greek philosopher, Socrates. The first step, as it is in the Alcoholics Anonymous 12-step program of recovery, is to know whether you have a problem. JC did not seek psychiatric help, because he did not think he had a mental health disorder. For many individuals in our society, mental health is a taboo subject, a sign of weakness and incompetence. Men especially are often reluctant to seek help for psychological issues.[18]

Past trauma and abuse may be too well hidden by defense mechanisms, keeping them out of mind even as they continue to cause pain. Like shrapnel that wasn't excised from the wound becomes encapsulated in scar tissue, untreated trauma may sit deep inside, causing pain that we barely notice, so used we are to it. It's worth asking oneself whether own mental health is a taboo thought; whether some past experiences are too painful to remember, and whether one can recognize the trauma they caused. Help is available. There are effective therapies, and pharmaceutical treatments. The first step, however, is to admit you have a problem.

One therapy that has been shown extremely helpful in reducing mental health disorders is cognitive-behavioral therapy (CBT).[19] The idea behind CBT is that people's internal narrative and their cognitions are often distorted. Simply put, that the stories they tell themselves are not true. For example, the voice inside may say, "I always do stupid stuff like this," or "I will never amount to anything." Both are likely to be distorted, because almost nothing is "always" one way or the other; and because nobody can know the future. The therapist works with the patient to first identify their distorted cognitions. Then the task of CBT is to effectively challenge the cognitions, with the help of the therapist, and eventually on one's own. Knowing one's internal narrator's tricks, it turns out, can be very helpful in avoiding their traps.

2. People need people. Social isolation may become routine, and instead of seeking company we might seek excuses or justifications for solitude. As Charles Bukowski said, "and when nobody wakes you up in the morning, and when nobody waits for you at night, and when you can do whatever you want, what do you call it, freedom or loneliness?" Nietzsche and Tesla called it freedom, but their mental health issues could have been eased had they sought a way out of isolation.

Psychotherapists who practice CBT often give patients "homework," assignments to do between sessions to address their unique cognitive distortions that contribute to their mental health problems. A common cognitive distortion is that they don't need other people, or that interactions with others are tiresome and distressing. But when patients intentionally go out of their way to have social interactions as part of their CBT homework, they often find themselves feeling better as a result.

Humans are social animals. No matter how creative or convincing our internal narrator can be in telling us that nobody loves us, that we are better off alone, or that our creative genius requires seclusion, we DO need people to thrive. In some ways, it is like drinking water. Sometimes we need to remember to do it, and do it intentionally, to avoid ill effects of dehydration. Just as we might wonder when was the last time we drank water, we might ask ourselves when was the last time we had a meaningful conversation with someone. And if it had been too long, perhaps it's time to call, or zoom, or meet. Instead of engaging in an internal soliloquy about why not or about how it might go wrong, it helps to ignore the internal narrator and "just do it," as the Nike ad says.

3. What is your normal? Things tend to become normal the more we are exposed to them. Even if it might seem extreme to someone else, to the person who is constantly berating themselves, or who is getting drunk every night, or who seeks out and shares disturbing and violent content online day in and day out, or spending all their time, energy, and money on gambling or pornography, the forest is lost for the trees. This is their normal. There is no natural stopping point—no flashing red light, no WARNING sign—no opportune moment to stop and make a different choice.

David Foster Wallace, in his 2005 commencement speech to the graduates of Kenyon College in Ohio, USA,[20] told a parable that has since become famous. Two young fish swim along, and come across an older fish swimming toward them. "Good morning, boys," says the older fish, "How's the water?" The two younger fish continue on their way a while, until one asks the other, "What the hell is water?"

The point Wallace made was to highlight how often things that make up our entire life are invisible to us. We are forever reaching for some goal, a thing, an achievement, a point in the future where we get something we think will make us happy, or important, or loved. In our heads, we run narratives and scenarios that spirit us away from the here and now. We mentally reshuffle conversations and events that have long ended, or plan for things that have not yet began—if they ever will—spinning, spinning, spinning stories that are just that. They are just stories. Meanwhile, our reality—our water—is lost to us.

What is your normal? Where does your best energy, your time, your resources go? What do you leave behind? What do you neglect? This is as good a moment as any to stop, and to consider your choices. This is as good a moment as any to make different ones.

Awareness of one's normal; of the content of the internal narrative; of one's needs for people, or needs for mental healthcare, this kind of awareness is not easy to master. But it is worth the effort. Empirical research shows that learning to maintain awareness through meditation, breathwork, and mindfulness is as effective as psychotherapy and more sustainable long-term, than pharmaceutical interventions for mental health disorders.[21,22] Mindfulness-building programs can also be effective in reducing extremism, and building resilience to political radicalization.[23] Today, mindfulness-based stress reduction (MBSR) programs are easily accessible online from any corner of the world, and they are very effective at building moment-to-moment awareness, reducing mental health issues, and reducing extremism.

King Solomon's wisdom. According to the Bible, King Solomon was the wisest man who ever lived. One day, he commissioned a ring with an engraving, to serve as a constant reminder. The engraving was to be just four words, but these four words would make a happy man sad, and a sad man happy. On his ring, King Solomon had the following phrase, "This, too, shall pass."

It is a reminder we can all use. Psychological research agrees with King Solomon's wisdom when it comes to emotions,[24] including the strongest ones, ones that make us want to shout off the rooftops, or strangle someone, or jump off a bridge. Emotions, research shows, are fleeting. They are unsettling for the body, flooding organs and tissues with chemicals that interfere with normal functioning. Proverbial butterflies in the stomach, sweaty palms, flexed muscles are not good for health. And so as soon as a strong emotion strikes, the body begins the work to return to the homeostasis, releasing chemicals to counteract the ones that the emotion caused. Opponent-process theory of emotion demonstrates that, no matter what the internal narrator says, no matter how convincing is the story that makes you mad, or sad, or angry—this, too, shall pass.[25] Knowing that, whether with help of a ring or without, can in itself reduce the extremity of emotions.

The singer-songwriter, Jewel, became a sensation with her debut album, Pieces of You, and has since sold over 30 million albums worldwide. But she started out with odds stacked sky-high against her. When Jewel was eight, her mother abandoned the family. Her father, suffering from undiagnosed PTSD, began to self-medicate by drinking heavily, and became abusive. At the age of 15, Jewel ran away from home. She worked odd jobs to make ends meet, and for a while was homeless in her teen years. She was severely depressed and anxious.

One day, Jewel wandered out to a cliff overlooking the Pacific Ocean, and sat on its edge for several hours, looking out at the ocean. The tide went out and then it came in again. In that Jewel saw a metaphor. Maybe, she thought, all the traumatic events she experienced in the past that haunted her still, all the frustrations and disappointments she experienced in the present—maybe these are like the tide that's out. And if they are like the tide, they are bound to turn. This thought, Jewel says, changed her life.

Whenever I get sad, depressed, stressed, anxious—I say to myself, "The tide is just out. I don't know how long it will take, but it will come back in because it has to: nothing is permanent." That's what I choose to think, at least.[26]

IN SUMMARY

Psychopathology is a form of personal extremism. Depression and anxiety often develop from negative self-talk and unfavorable comparisons of self to others, which have become ever more accessible through the internet and social media. Excessive dwelling on negative thoughts is a form of extremism; such rumination saps the ability to socialize and productively cope, and perpetuates the person's suffering. Online communities such as Incels or QAnon emphasize the hostility of the world outside of the community, alienating users and fostering high rates of mental illness among followers.

The good news is that effective therapies, such as cognitive-behavioral-therapy (CBT), help to moderate extreme thoughts and behaviors that cause suffering and emotional distress, which means that learning to moderate own extremism can nurture psychological resilience. Interestingly, what cognitive-behavioral therapies do is provide alternative, moderate narratives to address one's need for significance, to guard against maladaptive, perfectionist beliefs, such as "to be worthy I need to succeed at every task I attempt," or "to be worthy, I need to be liked by every person I meet." When feeling down, depressed, and desperate, extremism might beckon, yet it is well to resist its self-destructive siren call. Contemporary psychology affords a variety of well researched ways to rein in one's maladaptive tendencies; they are there for the asking, why not take advantage of what they have to offer?

NOTES

1 Dalgleish, T., Walsh, N. D., Mobbs, D., Schweizer, S., van Harmelen, A. L., Dunn, B., Dunn, V., Goodyer, I., & Stretton, J. (2017). Social pain and social

gain in the adolescent brain: A common neural circuitry underlying both positive and negative social evaluation. *Scientific Reports, 7*, 42010. https://doi .org/10.1038/srep42010

2   Quinn, D. M., & Stewart, A. M. (2019). Examining the racial attitudes of white pre-K–12 educators. *The Elementary School Journal, 120*(2), 272–299. https://doi.org/10.1086/705899

3   deLara, E. W. (2018). Consequences of childhood bullying on mental health and relationships for Young Adults. *Journal of Child and Family Studies, 28*(9), 2379–2389. https://doi.org/10.1007/s10826-018-1197-y

4   Hay, S. I., Okiro, E. A., Gething, P. W., Patil, A. P., Tatem, A. J., Guerra, C. A., & Snow, R. W. (2010). Estimating the global clinical burden of *Plasmodium falciparum* malaria in 2007. *PLoS Medicine, 7*(6), e1000290. https://doi.org /10.1371/journal.pmed.1000290

5   Hemelsoet, D., Hemelsoet, K., & Devreese, D. (2008). The neurological illness of Friedrich Nietzsche. *Acta Neurologica Belgica, 108*(1), 9–16. PMID: 18575181.

6   Hermitary. (2006). *Nietzsche on solitude—articles—House of solitude*. https://www .hermitary.com/solitude/nietzsche.html

7   NPR. (2009, January 4). Parting words: On solitude. NPR. https://www.npr .org/2009/01/04/98995429/parting-words-on-solitude#:~:text=Host %20Guy%20Raz%20offers%20parting,to%20cripple%20the%20creative %20mind.

8   Ölmez, S. B., & Youssef, N. A. (2022). Nikola Tesla: An autobiographical case study of trauma and resilience. *Epigenetics of Stress and Stress Disorders, 31*, 27–35. https://doi.org/10.1016/b978-0-12-823039-8.00009-5

9   Goldsmith, B. (2004). *Obsessive genius: The inner world of Marie Curie*. W. W. Norton & Company.

10 Markel, H. (2021, January 23). The day Marie Curie got snubbed by the French science world. PBS. https://www.pbs.org/newshour/science/the -day-marie-curie-got-snubbed-by-the-french-science-world

11 Moskalenko, S., González, J. F. G., Kates, N., & Morton, J. (2022). Incel ideology, radicalization and mental health: A survey study. *The Journal of Intelligence, Conflict, and Warfare, 4*(3), 1–29.

12 Moskalenko, S., Kates, N., González, J. F. G., & Bloom, M. (2022). Predictors of radical intentions among Incels: A survey of 54 self-identified Incels. *Journal of Online Trust and Safety, 1*(3).

13 Wahab, A. A., & Sakip, S. R. M. (2019). An overview of environmental design relationship with school bullying and future crime. *Environment-Behaviour Proceedings Journal, 4*(10), 11–18.

14 Fajmonová, V., Moskalenko, S., & McCauley, C. (2017). Tracking radical opinions in polls of US Muslims. *Perspectives on Terrorism*, 11(2), 36–48.

15 Moskalenko, S., Pavlović, T., & Burton, B. (2023). QAnon beliefs, political radicalization and support for January 6th insurrection: A gendered perspective. *Terrorism and Political Violence*, 1–20.

16 The Sportster. (2015, April 11). *Top 15 athletes who were bullied as children.* https://www.thesportster.com/entertainment/top-15-athletes-who-were-bullied-as-children/

17 Mancini, J. (2024, February 8). Elon Musk was bullied and tormented as a kid for being the "youngest and smallest guy," according to his mom—he worries his children "don't face enough adversity." *Yahoo! Finance.* https://finance.yahoo.com/news/elon-musk-bullied-tormented-kid-180216275.html

18 Lynch, L., Long, M., & Moorhead, A. (2018). Young men, help-seeking, and mental health services: Exploring barriers and solutions. *American Journal of Men's Health*, 12(1), 138–149.

19 Beck, A. T. (1991). Cognitive therapy: A 30-year retrospective. *American Psychologist*, 46(4), 368–375. https://doi.org/10.1037/0003-066X.46.4.368

20 Speeches with beautifully animated subtitles. (2018, December 26). *Animated subtitles | David Foster Wallace "this is water." (Beautiful subtitles to learn English).* [Video]. Youtube. https://www.youtube.com/watch?v=ms2BvRbjOYo

21 Vancampfort, D., Stubbs, B., Van Damme, T., Smith, L., Hallgren, M., Schuch, F., ... Firth, J. (2021). The efficacy of meditation-based mind-body interventions for mental disorders: A meta-review of 17 meta-analyses of randomized controlled trials. *Journal of Psychiatric Research*, 134, 181–191. 10.1016/j.jpsychires.2020.12.048

22 Chiesa, A., & Serretti, A. (2011). Mindfulness based cognitive therapy for psychiatric disorders: A systematic review and meta-analysis. *Psychiatry Research*, 187(3), 441–453. 10.1016/j.psychres.2010.08.011

23 Moskalenko, S. (2022). *Resilience to radicalization through mindfulness training.* United Nations Central Asian Conference, Doha, Qatar.

24 Solomon, R. L. (1980). The opponent-process theory of acquired motivation: The costs of pleasure and the benefits of pain. *American Psychologist*, 35(8), 691. https://doi.org/10.1037/0003-066X.35.8.691

25 Solomon, R. C. (Ed.). (2004). *Thinking about feeling: Contemporary philosophers on emotions.* Oxford University Press.

26 Oppenheimer, B. (2024b, June 3). Six at 6: Notes on "taste," what's hidden in plain sight, pure boredom, a thick accent, the tide, and this is water. *Billy Oppenheimer.* https://billyoppenheimer.com/june-2-2024/

7

EXTREMISM IN THE SOCIAL CONTEXT

Extremism, as we learned, happens when a given concern so dominates one's mind that all else fades and ceases to matter. In such
circumstances, anything that serves that focal concern appears legitimate, no holds barred. To be sure, the concern that overrides all others need not be social in nature. It could be physical or biological,
such as extreme hunger. The following true story makes this point.

On 13 October 1972, a chartered flight 571 of the Uruguayan
Air Force from Montevideo, Uruguay to Santiago, Chile, carrying
45 passengers and crew, crashed in the Andes mountains. Several of
the travelers died immediately on impact, and some died soon after
from their injuries. Search and rescue aircraft overflew the crash
site repeatedly in the days that followed, to no avail. Thus, all rescue
efforts were terminated after eight days of searching. In subsequent
72 days, the survivors faced extreme ordeals: sub-zero temperatures,
exposure, starvation, and an avalanche in which 13 additional passengers lost their lives.

Knowing that rescue efforts had been called off and facing certain
death from starvation, the survivors gave each other permission to
consume their bodies in case they died. Despite the horror and the
compunctions about eating the bodies of friends and relatives, all
who ultimately survived did so.

DOI: 10.4324/9781003472476-7

Realizing that everyone's death is assured unless rescue comes, two survivors, through a herculean effort, made their way into Chile and found help. Ultimately, they and 14 other survivors were saved and lived to tell their tale of horror.

Consuming bodies of friends and family is extreme in all senses of the term. It is a behavior outside the accepted norms of conduct everywhere, running counter to basic human inclinations, morally and aesthetically revolting, bordering on the unimaginable. Yet it can happen, as the story of flight 571 illustrates, when one need or concern, hunger in this instance, ascends to a level that trumps all else.

THE QUEST FOR SIGNIFICANCE

Any need elevated to a sufficient degree can motivate extreme activities, yet most extremisms we care about are social in nature and serve social needs. Foremost among those is the universal human need for respect and dignity, to be recognized and to matter; we call the striving to fulfill this need *the quest for significance*. Indeed, this quest more than any other fuels extremism. Because of its centrality, it is relatively easy to arouse the quest for significance and its pursuit.

Admittedly, not everyone is equally ambitious and determined to stand out. Some people, those with oversized egos, love to be the centers of attention. They crave "to be the baby at every christening, the bride at every wedding, and the corpse at every funeral" as Alice Longworth Roosevelt said of her father Theodore Roosevelt, the 26th president of the United States. Equally ambitious were many others who made history. Julius Caesar, for instance, was accused of excess ambition by a clique of Roman Senators who assassinated him for this "sin" on March 15, 44 BC. All monarchs named "the Great" (including Alexander, Peter, Katherine, Frederick, and other royal "Greats") were known for their oversized appetite for fame, as were Napoleon, Hitler, Putin, Donald Trump, and countless other women and men who shaped history.

Other people may be generally quiet and unassuming, shying away from the limelight, glad to be left alone. But when given the opportunity to do the right, worthy, thing, they might take action that brings them fame and admiration.

The story of Chiune Sugihara illustrates this point. Sugihara was a Japanese diplomat who served as a vice consul for the Japanese Empire in Kaunas, Lithuania. During World War II, Sugihara put his life and the lives of his family at risk by issuing approximately 6,000 life-saving transit visas to Jewish refugees, allowing them to flee Europe to the Orient.[1] Defying his pro-Nazi government that explicitly (and repeatedly) forbade him to do so, Sugihara wrote thousands of visas by hand over six weeks, working late into the night to near exhaustion. Even on the train heading back to Japan, he kept writing visas and throwing them out the window into the hands of the desperate refugees. Because of the immense risks he was taking on behalf of humanitarian values he cherished, Sugihara was an extremist in the true sense of the word.

Harriet Tubman, too, was an extremist for a good cause. An escaped slave from Maryland, she ventured to the North and became an abolitionist. At high risk to her life, she led hundreds of other slaves to freedom using a network of antislavery activists and safe houses known as the Underground Railroad. The knowledge she acquired through this activity made Tubman an invaluable source for information to the Union military in the Civil War. In fact, she was the first woman who led an armed expedition in the war, the Combahee Ferry Raid, liberating over 700 slaves in South Carolina.

Though the humanitarian motivations of Tubman and Sugihara may seem a far cry from those of ambitious conquerors like Julius Caesar or Napoleon, they share a common thread in driving people to accomplish something of value that will lend their lives social worth. Though not egocentric, both Tubman and Sugihara acted in the name of a value they wished to serve, helping others to freedom, which surely lent their lives much social merit and significance in their own and in others' eyes.

Extremism in the social context can thus take many forms, depending on the values whose affirmation through action gives one a sense of significance. This is illustrated by analyzing the motivation of terrorists, a topic we have both extensively studied in recent decades.

TERRORISTS' MOTIVATIONS

The question why terrorists carry out their despicable acts has puzzled researchers around the globe since terrorism rose to the center of the world's attention after 9/11/2001, when Al Qaeda extremists flew planes into the World Trade Center in New York City and the Pentagon, killing over 3,000 Americans. In response, social scientists have been proposing various motivations that may prompt people to join a terror group or embark on a terrorist mission. The proposals included among others vengeance, adoration of the leader, devotion to God, values sacred to one's group, and even feminism (the desire to prove that women too can be heroes devoted to a cause).

Now in deciphering a motivation for anything, it is important to distinguish between the end and the means. Both are important, yet they importantly differ: the end is the ultimate reason, *why* something occurred; the means is the activity undertaken to attain the end, *how* something occurred. Human motivation is driven by basic needs; these are the ultimate ends that any behavior aims to accomplish. Those ends are attained by a multitude of means, depending on culture, historical period, and circumstance.

The ultimate end that terrorism serves is, our research shows,[2] the fundamental human need for significance and mattering. In this sense, the various "motivations" for engaging in terrorism mentioned by scholars are but means to make the individual feel significant and worthy.

Take vengeance. Vengeance comes in response to humiliation. It aims to show the perpetrator that the erstwhile victim has the power to inflict harm, hence that they are significant and worthy of respect. Or take adoration of the leader: an action motivated by a desire to elicit the leader's approval which, in turn, would make one feel significant and worthy. The motivations to serve God, affirm one's group's sacred values, or promote feminism are also means to feeling good about oneself, having a sense that one has merit, signaling to oneself and others one's devotion to an ideal of virtue one's group cherishes.

How feelings of revenge and religious devotion can push one to extremism is illustrated by the story of Marwan Abu Ubeida, a young Iraqi militant, and a suicide terrorist in training at Abu Mussab al Zarqawi's insurgent group (the Attawhid, a precursor to ISIS). The scion of a wealthy Iraqi family, Marwan was drawn to Islamic studies and excelled in them, surpassing his four brothers in this domain. His first involvement with violent militancy occurred when in 2004 the American forces, in their attempt to quell an Iraqi protest in Fallujah, fired at a crowd of demonstrators of which Marwan was a part. Twelve people were killed, many more wounded, and Marwan foreswore to avenge them. Shortly, he and his friends got hold of weapons abandoned by the Iraqi army and opened fire on US soldiers who occupied a building in town. This was Marwan's initiation into a career of anti-American insurgency that culminated in his volunteering for a suicide mission.

The fight against the Americans and their supporters was couched in jihadist terms, giving Marwan a new sense of mission. After months of fighting as a foot soldier, he volunteered to become a suicide bomber, and finally, after a long wait, heard that he made the cut. On his account, this was the happiest day of his life. In an interview,[3] he vowed to be ready to die, to be looking forward to it, and praying for a large number of American casualties as a consequence of his mission. Along with other volunteers, he underwent a special program designed to discipline the mind and to cleanse the soul. He studied the lives of jihadists and listened to taped speeches about the rewards that await them in heaven. His thoughts were drawn to the "final stage" after a mission would be assigned to him. He hoped for an important one, directed perhaps by Zarqawi himself, and so maximally honorific and significance-affording. Marwan viewed this as the time of utmost exhilaration. He expected to be spending it in prayer and purification, preparing to meet Allah and receive a divine blessing for his deeds. "It doesn't matter whether people know what I did," he told his interviewer. "The only person who matters is Allah—and the only question he will ask me is 'How many infidels did you kill?'"

Religious fervor combined with a burning desire for revenge motivated the horrific suicide attack of Hanadi Jaradat, a 29-year-old lawyer from Jenin, a town in the West Bank of the River Jordan. On October 4th, 2003, she blew herself up in the Maxim restaurant in Haifa, co-owned by Arabs and Jews, causing the death of 21 people (Jews and Arabs), and the wounding of 51 others. What pushed an educated woman, charged with the responsibility of providing for her family, to perpetrate a massacre in which men, women, and children, all innocent civilians, some of her own ethnicity, were killed?

When she was 21, her fiancé, Abed al-Rahim Jaradat (a distant cousin) was killed by the Israel Defense Forces. The family's oldest son, Fadi, paid for her to attend law school, and she attended the Philadelphia University in Amman, Jordan. After graduating, she clerked for a year before finding employment in a law firm in Jenin. Her economic prospects and earning power were good. Things were looking up when in 2003, her cousin Saleh (34) and her beloved brother Fadi (24) were killed in front of her by Israeli security forces. In an interview with the Jordanian daily Al Arab al-Yaum she foreswore revenge:[4] "Your blood will not have been shed in vain," she said.

> The murderer will yet pay the price and we will not be the only ones who are crying. If our nation cannot realize its dream and the goals of the victims, and live in freedom and dignity, then let the whole world be erased.

The Israeli journalist Vered Levy-Barzilai gleaned information from diverse sources to depict Hanadi's background and personality. Like

Marwan, the Iraqi insurgent, Hanadi was deeply religious, always modestly dressed and spending hours on end in prayer and Qu'ranic study. Her piety and religious devotion intensified after the death of her brother. She was disconsolate, and increasingly given to religious asceticism. She fasted as one does during Ramadan well before Ramadan commenced.

During the mourning period after the death of Fadi, Hanadi was visited by members of the Islamic Jihad's women's movement. Likely, on this occasion, the idea of her suicide attack originated.

Both Marwan and Hanadi were driven to self-sacrificial extremism by the humiliation they suffered at the hands of their people's enemies (i.e. Americans and Israelis, respectively). They felt that the value of their social identity was tarnished by their detractors. Hence their desire for revenge that would level the playing field and demonstrate their power to those who stripped their honor.

Murdering innocents is contrary to the basic human tendencies of empathy and compassion. How could people bring themselves to carry out such horrific deeds? It is here that the religious justification comes in. The idea that violence is demanded by God and that it represents a holy war against God's enemies removes doubt, guilt, and compunction about the mass killing that a suicide attack aims to accomplish.

At times, the loss of significance that motivates extremism comes from one's personal sense of inadequacy and worthlessness. A person raised in a religious family who became secular and flouted religious prohibitions, for instance, may feel guilty and unwholesome about their transgressions. In moments of personal crisis, such individuals may be particularly drawn to religiously couched extremist narratives that promise redemption. The story of Hayat Boumeddiene, who aided and abetted the January 2014 attack on the Charlie Hebdo magazine in Paris, where 12 people lost their lives, exemplifies this psychological dynamic.

Boumeddiene was married to Amedy Coulibaly who, in parallel to the Kouachi brothers' attack on Charlie Hebdo, fatally shot a policewoman in a Paris street and killed four people at a kosher grocery before being himself killed by the police.

Boumeddiene didn't have an easy life. She was only 8 when her mother died of a heart ailment, didn't get along with her step-mother, and was therefore placed in a group home with an Algerian family, a "house of nonbelievers" as her highly religious father Mohamed Boumeddiene described it. Hayat became Westernized and nonreligious, sporting a black bikini in a photo with her husband during a vacation in the Dominican Republic. The incongruity between her secular lifestyle and the religiousness of her original upbringing must have weighed heavily on Boumeddiene. It was at that time that she met Djamel Benghal, a top Al Qaeda recruiter, who introduced her and her husband to the fundamentalist, violence-promoting version of Islam. "I had a difficult past, and religion answered all my questions and brought me peace," she told the police during an early interrogation.[5]

And essential element of the religious narrative that Boumeddiene adopted was the utter justifiability of violence against the West. In a 2010 interview, Boumeddiene said, "When I see innocent people massacred in Palestine, Iraq, Chechnya, Afghanistan where Americans send bombs and all that – and they're not terrorists? ...When American kill innocent people... it is of course justifiable that men should take arms to defend their wives and children."[6] Boumeddiene fled France a day before the Charlie Hebdo attack, and as of this writing is considered one of the most wanted fugitives in Europe.

War. War is the epitome of an extreme state, in which masses of people sacrifice their own lives and take the lives of countless others in suppression of their own feelings of empathy and compassion to fellow human beings. As of this writing, two major wars are raging, making headlines and attracting the world's attention: The Russian large-scale invasion of Ukraine, now in its second year in which, according to the *New York Times*, 500,000 people were killed or wounded[6], and the Israel-Hamas war, in which as of this writing 2,000 Israelis[7] and 36,000 Palestinians[8] reportedly lost their lives. Both these wars and many others originate from leaders' quest for significance that they attempt to satisfy through aggression meant to deliver them the glory of victory.

The Russian invasion of Ukraine is the brainchild of Vladimir Putin, the dictatorial president of Russia. His outsized ambition is legendary and longstanding. When the Soviet Union fell apart in 1991, most Russian officials in St. Petersburg's mayor's office were quick to replace the portraits of the Communist revolutionary heroes Vladimir Lenin and Sergei Kirov with the portrait of Boris Yeltsin, the new Russian president. There was one exception, however. The mayor's personal assistant, young Vladimir Putin, chose for his wall a portrait of Peter the Great: one of Russia's most important czars, who made Russia into an empire. This incident now seems like an omen. It bears on an aspect of Putin that 30 years later has made him the alarming center of global attention.

Vladimir Vladimirovich Putin soared on the scene of Russian politics at a propitious moment. The humiliated loser of the Cold War, the USSR in 1991 saw its vast empire that encompassed much of Eastern Europe quickly coming unglued. For many Russians, it was a cultural trauma that lasted for decades. In 2005, Putin, by that time reelected as Russia's president, proclaimed that the collapse of the Soviet Union was "the greatest geopolitical catastrophe of the century."[9] He saw it as a profound loss of significance, a precipitous fall from greatness.

The loss of empire and world status called on Putin to reverse that disaster, and thus restore Russian greatness (and achieve his own, like Peter I). The devastating war in Ukraine was just one consequence of Putin's imperial ambitions, along with wars that Russia waged under his leadership in Chechnya, Georgia, as well as military interventions in Syria, Central African Republic, Mali, and Burkina Faso[10].

In a different way, the Israeli-Palestinian war in Gaza is also a case of extremism prompted by the struggle for significance. Erroneously, the Israeli-Palestinian conflict is typically perceived as "realistic," in which the parties vie for a concrete scarce resource, in this instance the territory of Palestine. We submit, however, that the land here is but a proxy, a means to an ultimate psychological end, the feelings of significance and mattering over which Israelis and Palestinians are locked in a deadly struggle. Throughout history, land and territory have been the hallmarks of national pride and glory. Ruling vast lands and their inhabitants has motivated conquests, imperialisms, and expansionisms from antiquity to the present.

Land, as such, is a fungible commodity interchangeable with cash; in fact, it was sold in large quantities by Palestinian Arabs to Jewish immigrants to Palestine in the first half of the 20th century. But land's symbolic value as a means to significance cannot be replaced by material means.[11] Understanding this holds the key to resolving the conflict, and envisioning the circumstances in which it might be possible to attain this elusive end.

In the early 20th century, when the seeds of the conflict were sowed, both European Jews, who fled from Europe to Palestine, and local Palestinian Arabs were waking up to a new opportunity to enhance their significance and mattering that for centuries has been badly wanting. The nationalist spirit that swept the international order, which started at the end of the 19th century and culminated at the conclusion of World War I, beckoned to both Palestinian Arabs and Jews who, for different reasons, felt downtrodden and humiliated. The national awakening of both peoples was thus intertwined and concurrent. Like other Middle Eastern, primarily Arab peoples, the Palestinians were under colonial dominion that lasted for centuries, including the Ottoman Empire that ruled Palestine for some 400 years and Great Britain that took over Palestine at the end of World War I. Consequently, when new Arab countries, such as Saudi Arabia, Iraq, and Jordan, were being carved out of the collapsing Ottoman Empire, the Palestinian Arabs too sought to obtain a country of their own.

At the same time, virulent antisemitism in Europe reached new heights. Publications such as the Protocols of the Elders of Zion, which first appeared in 1903 in Russia, generated theories of an international Jewish conspiracy. These fomented waves of massacres of Jews across all Eastern Europe and in Russia in particular (the infamous "pogroms"). Feeling unwanted anywhere, the Jews concluded that they must have a state of their own and that the only place on earth fit for that purpose is in their ancestral land of Israel—then called Palestine.

Swept by the general nationalist worldview that dominated the political discourse of the time, Arab and Jewish forms of nationalism emerged, separately and in parallel, as a ray of hope to both beleaguered peoples, promising them liberation from constraints that deprived them of significance and dignity. Tragically, the promised way out of their misery brought them into a deadly conflict with each other, which has been reverberating until the present time.

Even though both parties to the Palestinian-Israeli conflict entered it aiming for significance gain, both ended up with substantial significance losses. The Palestinians suffered decades of occupation, a vast loss of life, and the devastation that the 2023–24 Gaza war brought. The Israelis too experienced profound indignities over the years: in the 1973 Yom Kippur war, the two uncontrollable intifadas, and the nightmare of the October 7, 2023, massacre. By adopting the "winner takes all" attitude, extremists on both sides have been squandering opportunities for significance gains that peace would afford: dignity that comes from achievements in economic, artistic, or scientific spheres, and from sparing future generations the horrors and travails of endless war.

A matter of values. As we have seen, the quest for significance and mattering can motivate both humanitarian actions of protecting others and saving them from harm, and violent actions aimed at destroying others. In both cases, individuals are motivated to gain the respect of self and others, the sense that they matter and are worthy, significant persons. Yet how they do it couldn't differ more. Why? The answer, discussed in Chapter 5, lies in the narratives that tell people *how* to attain significance in given circumstances. Such narratives in turn are grounded in values that the society of which the individual is member holds dear.

Any society typically holds on to different values that are salient and dominant in a different context. A society at war highlights the values of courage, fortitude, and aggressiveness directed at the group's enemies. A society at peace may stress achievements in science, arts, business, or sports.

A striking example of an extremist for science was Marie Sklodowska-Curie, the two-time Nobel Prize winner, in physics and in chemistry, for the discoveries of radium and polonium. Maria Sklodowska-Curie was born in 1867 into a family of educators and scientists in the Kingdom of Poland, which at the time was part of the Russian empire. As a woman, Sklodowska-Curie was prevented from being admitted to a regular university, opting therefore to pursue her studies at the clandestine Flying University, a Polish patriotic institution of higher learning that admitted women students. In 1891 she left Poland for France and pursued the studies of physics, chemistry, and mathematics at the University of Paris. Her resources were meager, and her apartment cold, so she kept herself warm by wearing all the clothes she had, layering them like cabbage leaves. She studied so hard that she sometimes forgot to eat, working from dawn till night, studying by day and tutoring younger students in the evenings. She finally enrolled for a doctorate at the University of Paris, and received it in 1903, the same year in which she was awarded the first of her two Nobel Prizes, this one with her husband Pierre Curie. The award money allowed the Curies to hire their first laboratory assistant.

Marie Sklodowska-Curie sacrificed much for her scientific work, and much of her career was marred by xenophobia, sexism, and poor working conditions. The Curies did not have a dedicated laboratory; most of their research was carried out in a converted shed next to ESPCI (Ecole Superieure de Physique et de Chimie Industrielles de la Ville de Paris). The shed, formerly a medical school dissecting room, was poorly ventilated and not even waterproof. According to her biographer, she lived "in a world quite removed from human beings,"[12] spent all her time in the lab, and experienced recurrent bouts of depression. She died on 4 July 1934, at the age of 66, from aplastic anemia apparently caused by her long-term exposure to radiation.

Did Sklodowska-Curie care about her significance or was she exclusively concerned about her science? There is evidence that she indeed cared about being recognized and given credit for her outstanding work. She was aware of the importance of promptly publishing her discoveries and[13] thus establishing her priority[14]. And in her biography of her husband, she noted twice the fact that her ideas about radioactive substances were her own (rather than his), leaving no room for ambiguity in this regard. Indeed, in those early years of the 20th century, many scientists would find it difficult to believe that a woman could be capable of the groundbreaking work she was carrying out.

Art and sacrifice. The idea that artists make great sacrifices for their art is central to the concept of the "starving artist" exemplified by such artistic giants like Rembrandt who died penniless. Similarly, Amedeo Modigliani, a Jewish Italian painter died of tuberculosis in an unheated apartment in Paris in 1920, battling addictions to drugs and alcohol and frustrated with his lack of success. His common law wife, Jeanne Hebuterne, committed suicide the following year, leaping to her death while pregnant with their child.

Like Modigliani, Vincent Van Gogh left the comforts of a middle-class life for his art, at which he ultimately considered himself a failure. This likely contributed to the misery and torment he suffered during his painting career. Lonely, unsuccessful, his only meaningful connection being with his younger brother Theo, he suffered repeated bouts of mental illness and depression for which he was treated in mental hospitals. In a fit of rage caused by what apparently was a spat with Paul Gauguin, a fellow painter, he cut off his ear. Though worried about his mental stability, he often neglected his physical health, did not eat properly, and drank heavily. Finally at the age of 37, he died by suicide.

Michelangelo was another extremist for art, euphoric when carving marble and suffering when prevented from doing so. As his famous biographer, Irving Stone, attests, Michelangelo often worked for up to 20 hours a day, barely eating and sleeping, and going long periods of time without bathing or even changing his clothes. He wore a special candle-holder hat so that he could carve through the night. Anti-social in the extreme, he was fixated in his opinions, and argued vociferously with his patrons, who complained about his explosive temperament.

These three examples of suffering artists are a mere "drop in a bucket" among many similar cases. But the point is this: though the lives and circumstances of Michelangelo, Van Gogh, and Modigliani couldn't be more different, what they had in common, and what characterizes many great artists, is single-mindedness, a sense of purpose, and an unswerving commitment to their projects for which they were ready to sacrifice all else—in short, extremism.

Their passion stemmed from the hope to create something important, making them feel they matter, that their life had meaning, social worth and significance. Though not always recognized in their lifetime, the conviction that they were onto something worthwhile gave them the strength to keep going and find glimmers of ecstasy among torrents of agony and misery. As Van Gogh stated in a letter to his brother, Theo, "*I can't change the fact that my paintings don't sell. But the time will come when people will recognize that they are worth more than the value of the paints used in the picture.*" [15] The rest of course is history.

IN SUMMARY

Though any human need can be elevated to great heights, legitimizing extreme action, the universal human quest for significance and mattering is the main force behind diverse types of extremism in the social sphere. Depending on cultural narratives about paths to significance, this quest can motivate extreme humanism, artistic excellence, momentous scientific discoveries—but also unleash terrorism, brutality, and war. Our capacity for extremism is a fixed given, part of our human nature. The challenge is to channel it in positive pro-social directions and to avoid the temptation to seek significance through the destruction of others.

NOTES

1 The World Holocaust Remembrance Center. (n.d.). *Chiune Sempo sugihara*. Yad Vashem. https://www.yadvashem.org/righteous/stories/sugihara.html

2 Kruglanski, A. W., Bélanger, J. J., Gelfand, M., Gunaratna, R., Hettiarachchi, M., Reinares, F., Orehek, E., Sasota, J., & Sharvit, K. (2013). Terrorism—A (self) love story: Redirecting the significance quest can end violence. *American Psychologist*, 68(7), 559–575. https://doi.org/10.1037/a0032615; Kruglanski, A. W., Chen, X., Dechesne, M., Fishman, S., & Orehek, E. (2009). Fully committed: Suicide bombers' motivation and the quest for personal significance. *Political Psychology*, 30(3), 331–357. https://doi.org/10.1111/j.1467–9221.2009.00698.x.

3 Ghosh, B. (2005, June 26). Inside the mind of an Iraqi suicide bomber. *Time Magazine*. https://time.com/archive/6673814/inside-the-mind-of-an-iraqi-suicide-bomber/

4 Abufarha, N. (2020). *The making of a human bomb: An ethnography of Palestinian resistance*. Duke University Press.; Maximilian. (February 5, 2023). The story of Hanadi Jaradat. *Medium*. https://medium.com/@m4xim1l1an/the-story-of-hanadi-jaradat-70049bedd182

5 Birnbaum, M., & Mekhennet, S. (2015, February 2). Hayat Boumeddiene, wife of Paris attacker, becomes France's most-wanted woman. *The Washington Post*. https://washingtonpost.com/world/europe/wife-of-paris-attacker-now-frances-most-wanted-woman/2015/02/02/b03c6950-a7da-11e4-a162-121d06ca77f1_story.htm

6 Cooper, H., Gibbons-Neff, T., Schmitt, E., & Julian E. B. (2023, August 18). Troop deaths and injuries in Ukraine war near 500,000, U.S. officials say. *The New York Times*. https://www.nytimes.com/2023/08/18/us/politics/ukraine-russia-war-casualties.html?smid=url-share

7 Al-salam, A. A. (2024, March 12). As armed men surround trucks, Gazans blame Israel, Hamas for humanitarian aid crisis. *Jerusalem Post*. https://www.jpost.com/israel-hamas-war/article-791412

8 Presse, A. F. (2024, June 3). Health Ministry in Hamas-run Gaza says war death toll at 36, 479. *Barron's*. https://www.barrons.com/news/health-ministry-in-hamas-run-gaza-says-war-death-toll-at-36-479-09712962

9 *Russian President Putin's State of the Nation Address* (2005, April 25). https://irp.fas.org/news/2005/04/putin042505.html

10 Galeotti, M. (2022). *Putin's wars: From Chechnya to Ukraine*. Bloomsbury Publishing.

11 Atran, S., & Axelrod, R. (2008). Reframing sacred values. *Negotiation Journal*, 24(3), 221–246. https://doi.org/10.1111/j.1571–9979.2008.00182.x

12 Goldsmith, B. (2005). *Obsessive genius: The inner world of Marie Curie* (pp 59–60). W.W. Norton & Company.

13 Goldsmith, B. (2005). *Obsessive genius: The inner world of Marie Curie* (pp. 59–60). W.W. Norton & Company.

14 UMCS. (n.d.). *Biography of Maria Curie-Skłodowska*. https://www.umcs.pl/en/biography-of-maria-curie-sklodowska,24559.htm

15 Bakker, N., Jansen, L., & Luijten, H. (2020). *Vincent van Gogh: A life in letters*. Thames & Hudson; *712: To Theo Van Gogh. Arles, on or about Thursday, October 25, 1888*. 712 (717, 557): To Theo van Gogh. Arles, on or about Thursday, October 25, 1888.—Vincent van Gogh Letters. (n.d.). https://www.vangoghletters.org/vg/letters/let712/letter.html#translation

8

LOVE'S EXTREMES

Here we turn, for a change, to the good news about extremism, its constructive side. Love, the queen of all positive interpersonal emotions, as it turns out, is the prototypical instance of extremism. Take romantic love, one of the most celebrated aspects of the human experience, the subject of literature, plays, movies, and visual arts for centuries. Falling in love is an extreme state in which the person's attention and resources are focused on the loved one to the exclusion of other (arguably more rational) pursuits. Throughout time and across the land, myths and fairytales, sonnets and songs, stories and paintings extol romantic love as one of humanity's favorite extremisms.

Great love is often portrayed as an obsession, an inescapable and relentless state of mind that yearns for complete togetherness with the object of one's desire. Every love song, from ballads sung to mandolins under moonlit balconies to chart-topping rock, pop, or country, professes love along similar lines. You're all I need, you're all I ever wanted, I can't live without you, I'd jump on a grenade for you, I'd walk a thousand miles and cross a hundred oceans just to be with you. Day and night, here and there and everywhere, the songs say, all the thoughts, all the hopes and desires are focused on the object of one's infatuation. The Bard himself, William Shakespeare, had a thing or two to say about love as well. They, too, reflected the obsessive, all-encompassing state of mind that is love:

DOI: 10.4324/9781003472476-8

My love is as a fever, longing still
For that which longer nurseth the disease,
Feeding on that which doth preserve the ill,
Th' uncertain sickly appetite to please.
My reason, the physician to my love,
Angry that his prescriptions are not kept,
Hath left me, and I desperate now approve
Desire is death, which physic did except.

(Sonnet 147)

LOVING EXTREMELY MUCH

Romantic love takes over one's thoughts and desires, it keeps one up at night, it makes one forget food and rest in pursuit of their passion, it makes one do foolish, crazy things. England's King Edward VIII, for example, fell in love with a twice-divorced American woman, Wallis Simpson. This was already ill-advised for the British monarch, but King Edward did not stop there. When the British political institutions made it clear that the relationship would not be accepted or recognized, King Edward abdicated the throne to be with his beloved, having reigned less than a year.[1] Over 30 years later, in 1970, Edward said in an interview with BBC that he did not regret the decision.

But it does not take a king to fall crazy in love—or to do crazy things for love. As Edward Dyer's poem says, "and love is love, in beggars as in kings." Consider Niko Pirosmani, a Georgian primitivist painter at the turn of the 20th century. Pirosmani was struggling to sell his art, often painting store signs in exchange for food. In 1909, a famous French actress Marguerite de Sevres came to perform in Tiflis (Tbilisi), the capital of Georgia. Her beauty and talent attracted many men, and Pirosmani was smitten. But De Sevres stayed cool and distant. She became annoyed when Pirosmani, clad in his worn-out clothes, tearfully professed his love, fell to his knees and kissed the ground she walked on. So, on his birthday, Pirosmani sold all his possessions, including his house, and used the money to buy all the flowers in the city. He arranged for multiple carts to be laden with roses, lilacs, and tulips, to deliver the flowers to the hotel where the actress stayed, and to unload them onto the square at night. By morning, a heavenly aroma filled the air. The actress woke up to a flower-covered square outside her windows. She ran out of the hotel, and gave Pirosmani her first and last kiss. The same day, De Sevres left town; Pirosmani never saw her again[2]. The painter died poor. After his death, his art gained popularity, and is highly valued today. One of his most important paintings is "Actress Marguerite."

You might know Robert Louis Stevenson as the author of *Treasure Island* and *Strange Case of Dr Jekyll and Mr Hyde*. Stevenson's best story, however, was not fictional but real. Since childhood, Stevenson suffered from a lung ailment that left him sickly and gaunt. At 26, he was traveling through France with a friend when he met an American family: the married mother, Francis (Fanny) Osborn, was 11 years his senior. She was vacationing with her 16-year-old daughter and 9-year-old son. Stevenson fell in love with Fanny, but their acquaintance was formal and brief. Soon, Fanny and the children returned home to San Francisco, and broken-hearted Stevenson went back to Scotland. Eleven months after their meeting, Fanny wrote Stevenson a letter, revealing that she was gravely ill. That was all he needed to embark on an extreme course of action.

Even though his family and friends were vociferously against the romance with a much older married woman halfway across the world, Stevenson scraped together enough money for the cheapest ticket to cross the ocean. The long journey on the lower decks of an ocean liner took a toll on his fragile health. On top of that, upon disembarking in California, Stevenson caught malaria. Barely recovered, still weak, Stevenson continued his journey. He did not find Fanny at her last address in San Francisco, learning that she had moved without leaving a letter for him or a mailing address. That did not deter him. With some difficulty, he found out that her new location was Monterrey. Denying himself food, Stevenson used what little money he had to buy a ticket for an overcrowded train; then he got a horse and rode; then walked to get to his beloved.

Malnourished and barely alive, Stevenson made it. Eventually and through great trials and tribulations, Fanny got divorced, and the pair got married in 1880. Already in 1881, Stevenson wrote his first novel, *Treasure Island*, and continued a successful writing career and a happy marriage until his sudden death from stroke at the age of 44[3]. Against the wishes of his family, despite his weak health, using every bit of what little money and energy he had, Stevenson directed all his resources to his goal of reaching the woman he loved. It took him months and almost cost him his life, but the extremism paid off at the end, and the happiness in love inspired his writing.

Love's extremisms led people to abdicate the throne, to turn all their worldly possessions into a giant bouquet, to pursue their love to the last dime and the last breath. People have killed and died, created and destroyed for love. Why does love inspire such extremism?

THE PSYCHOLOGICAL BASES OF LOVE'S EXTREMES

Feeling good about oneself. One answer is the subjective experience of love. As Victor Hugo said in *Les Misérables*, "The supreme happiness of life consists in the conviction that one is loved; loved for one's own sake—let us say rather, loved in spite of one's self." We do crazy things for love because the experience, or even the hope of being loved in return by someone one sees as amazing and adorable, makes one feel special to the utmost, a truly "chosen" one. That is why love is often described as the pinnacle of human experience, the best feeling there is, life's greatest ecstasy.

Brain functions. Love's extremism is enabled by specific neural and hormonal processes. Neuroscience finds that the brains of people in love function remarkably similarly to those of people in the grip of a substance addiction.[4] Neurologically, we crave time with our loved ones the same way a heroin addict craves a hit. When in their presence, our brain releases the same chemical, dopamine, as an addict's brain releases when they use the addictive substance. We feel the same kind of euphoria, relief, and pleasure in the arms of a loved one as a cocaine addict after snorting a line. We suffer the same withdrawal when separated from our loved one, marked by the same corticotropin-releasing factors in the lovers' brains as in addicts' brains when they can't "score." Neurologically, it makes no difference whether the "score" is a date or a kiss, a shot of vodka or a puff of crack.

> Addicts are also willing to sacrifice in order to obtain and consume drugs; however, those exact same self-sacrificing behaviors that we see as romantic and laudable in the context of parental or romantic love are seen as dangerous and self-destructive in the context of drug addiction.[5]

In short, love is similar to a drug, and to fall in love is to develop a kind of addiction in which being with and getting the affection of one's beloved is all that matters. "All you need is love" famously sang the Beatles. For the enamored ones, nothing could ring truer.

How we evolved. Evolutionary psychologists have a theory about why this biological mechanism would evolve to render its "victims" proverbial fools in love[6]. Ironically, the cause for love's foolishness is our extreme intelligence; more specifically, the big brains that evolved to support it. Other animals, kittens or puppies, are born far more independent than human babies. Deer fawns or lion cubs are able to get around and seek food and shelter for themselves days after birth. But humans' ginormous head, housed in a correspondingly huge skull, required a biological compromise between the mother's ability to birth the baby through the pelvic bones and the baby's ability to survive outside the womb. Too big a head for a baby, no matter how advantageous after birth, would mean death for the mother, and thus a likely demise of the baby as well. The result of these competing evolutionary pressures was that human babies are born relatively premature: completely dependent on their mothers, needing around-the-clock care for years before they can achieve the independence that comes naturally to newborn offspring of less intellectually advanced species.

And because a pregnant woman or a mother caring for an infant needs care of her own, especially in the harsh environments of our ancestors, where food, shelter, and safety were hard-won, human babies have a greater chance of surviving into adulthood if they have two people caring for them: a mother and a father.[7] Those babies who had the benefit of a pair of human caretakers in the early stages of development are far more likely to survive to adulthood and have kids of their own, propagating the genes of their coupled parents, than babies whose parents were apart. Natural selection, then, would favor and multiply genes that fostered coupling.

Coupling, you might say, is not love. Why not have all the benefits and none of the costs of romantic love by evolving pragmatic coupling? Why all the craziness of love?

As evolutionary psychologists point out, having a baby is a commitment that "costs" a great deal more to women than it does to men. In years of reproductive life, in resources needed to birth and nurse, in risks to health and attractiveness to other partners, having a baby is much harder on a woman than on a man. And if a woman picks a partner who would desert her to care for the child alone, reducing the child's chances of survival, the woman's evolutionary resources would be wasted. It is thus extremely important for a woman to choose a partner who would stay devoted to her and potential future children. For men, on the other hand, the most pragmatic (and evolutionarily advantageous) approach is not to get bogged down with a single woman, but rather to impregnate as many as possible while taking care of none. For actual coupling to take place, therefore, the woman must somehow overcome suspiciousness, and the man must overcome cynicism. Without the ability to know the future, how would a woman know that a partner would stay? How would a man give up the many other fish in the sea? The answer to this dilemma, according to evolutionary psychologists, is love.[8]

Honest signaling. Because romantic love is very much like an addiction, because it makes the person do seemingly crazy things: give up sleep, food, and most prized possessions, because it makes them believe, irrationally, that there is nobody in the world more beautiful, or smart, or funny than their beloved, and never ever will be, love is an *honest signal*. An honest signal is a biological marker that is very hard to fake and thus easy to believe. Like peacock's brilliant plumage or a silverback gorilla's huge muscles signal good health, romantic love's biological symptoms signal commitment. Seeing all the foolishness of the partner in love, the woman can believe that the man is going to stick around, and the man that no other woman is worth his attention. This allows for the pair to bond and stay together, giving their potential future children a better chance of survival.

Supporting this theory, research on the duration of romantic love, the kind that results in chemical imbalance in the brain, that manifests as insomnia, anorexia, obsessive thoughts, and compulsive actions, found that it tends to last somewhere between 18 months and 3 years[9]—just the amount of time it takes to have a baby, and have a baby turn into a far more sustainable age of toddlerhood. The extremism of romantic love tends to have a shelf life consistent with the time needed to support human children in their most vulnerable age. Among our ancestors, those who were genetically programmed to feel love were more likely to successfully pair, convincing their partners that they were "all in." They were also more likely to provide the resources needed for their offspring's survival, ensuring that their romantic genes outperformed the cynical genes of their cooler-headed contemporaries, leaving us a genetic legacy of love.

But that's not all that the love circuits in our brain do for extremism. As extreme as romantic love can be, there is another kind that is far more extreme, and longer-lasting. The love of a mother for her child is possibly the greatest and also most prevalent case of positive, pro-social extremism.

MATERNAL LOVE

A newborn baby is nothing but trouble. Day and night they need, need, need: food, shelter, warmth, quiet, clean diapers, to be held, to be put to sleep, to be entertained, and often some *je ne sais quoi*—something impossible to figure out, yet which requires urgent attention and intervention. The stakes are literally life and death, because human babies are fragile. Their skulls are not hardened yet, they can't regulate temperature, don't have immune systems of their own, can't run or hide from danger, can't feed themselves. If the mother does not take good care of them around the clock, depriving herself of everything to cater to their needs, the baby will fall easy prey to predators, accidents, malnutrition, starvation, hypothermia, and an unimagined variety of other life-threatening dangers. And if a woman gives birth and the baby dies, she loses at least 10 months of her reproductive lifespan, which is limited to about 3 decades, from puberty to menopause. That's a cost that puts negligent or indifferent mothers at an evolutionary disadvantage. The extremist mothers' loving genes are thus far more likely to be represented in the future generations.

Maternal love extreme not only in the amount of resources it takes, but also in the kinds of lengths to which a mother would go to protect her child. Not only in humans, but in other animals, too, the period of child-rearing is associated with heightened vigilance and easily provoked aggression.[10] Maternal aggression in mammals is mediated by the hormones that are released when the mother is nursing the young: prolactin and oxytocin.[11] Maternal aggression is the reason park rangers advise never to stand between a bear and her cubs. A "mama bear" who believes her young ones are endangered will fight tooth and nail to protect them. And because human babies take far longer to mature and require far more resources than other mammals, both human parents feel strong love for them, with fathers often as willing to fight and die to protect children as well as mothers.

The good news about extremism, then, is that it is the very thing that makes human life possible. If it wasn't for the extremism of love, romantic and parental, our species would not exist. Extreme love is at the cradle of humanity. We partake of extremism with mother's milk. We are all its beneficiaries, the carriers of the genes that gave rise to it in generations of our ancestors and continue to arouse it today.

NEW WINE, OLD WINESKINS

And here's the thing about the brain structures that evolved over millennia to facilitate extreme love: humanity's world was very different thousands of years ago. There were no nations, no armies. There were no ethnic groups. There were no industries, and no careers, no sports teams, no political parties to root for. All of these entities that inspire extremism in today's world are relatively new. Whereas the brain structures we have in place are relatively old. There has not been enough time to evolve separate structures to deal with all the novelties. Instead, our brains repurpose the old mechanisms to deal with the new world.

We call our nations motherlands or fatherlands, and we devote the kind of resources to their continued survival that our ancestors reserved for kin. Soldiers develop a "bond stronger than brothers," and sacrifice for that brotherly love. Christians pray to "Our father who art in heaven" and Catholics call Virgin Mary "our mother." Jews believe they are all family, part of the original 12 tribes of Israel. People devote themselves to their career, or to their favorite sports team, or to their political party—giving up their time, sleep, and energy the same way that lovers and parents do.

Religious cults indoctrinate their members by having them give up on their actual families and social circles, and at the same time redefining the family as the cult, often with the cult leader as a godlike father.[12] Providing both the network and the narrative, cult recruiters capitalize on human capacity for extreme and selfless love, redirecting it away from followers' actual children to the cult. The same process can be observed in the indoctrination of child soldiers, who are often orphaned by the very people who then tell them the military is their new family.[13]

And if something threatens what we love, if our family is in danger or our nation is under attack, if our religion is persecuted, if our political party is humiliated or our business requires round the clock care to stay afloat, well then we give our energy, our time, our resources, and sometimes our lives to protect it. We fight for the things we love the only way our brain knows how: the way a person in love fights to be with their loved one, or the way a parent fights to protect their child. It is possible that all extremism is rooted in human capacity to love, repurposing the mental structure that evolved for sustaining human life.

Perhaps it is hard to consider this possibility when thinking about violent extremists, whose actions seem much less inspired by love than by hate. Except, what looks like offense to us they construe as defense, a fight for something they hold dear that they feel is in dire straits. For Osama bin Laden, this cherished threatened ideal was the Umma—the nation of Islam he felt was being corrupted and defiled by the depraved West. For environmental terrorists, it is mother nature they feel is choking to death on corporate greed.

Radical movements often tell narratives of imminent threat—to incite defensive hatred and violence against those who they claim are the malefactors, in the same way that a mama bear becomes aggressive when she believes her cubs are in danger. QAnon tells of kidnapped children sexually abused in basements and dungeons by the cabal of evil Democrats. Right-Wing groups tell of the Great Replacement—Black and Brown people subjugating Whites. Russian propaganda talks of Ukrainian biolabs dispatching deadly viruses via migratory birds and insects to infect and kill Russians. Terrorism or violent extremism is an expression of protective care by those who love these entities[14]—the Umma, the environment, children, White people, Russians—and who believe these narratives of imminent threat.

Historically, disinformation narratives that resulted in extreme violence against a group they targeted tended to describe horrors the target group inflicted on the children of one's community.[15] Witch hunts in Europe were inspired by a disgraced clergyman's book, The Witch's Hammer, which detailed torture and killing of kidnapped children by Devil-worshipping women. The result was tens of thousands of women murdered across Europe by those who believed the story. Jews in the Russian empire suffered a wave of deadly pogroms because of a czarist-police-produced fake document, The Protocols of the Elders of Zion, which claimed that Jews steak gentile children and ritualistically drink their blood. Romani were also persecuted and mass murdered in Europe because of disinformation that they steal gentile children. Extremism is perhaps easiest to inspire by narratives that threaten children because protecting children is the primordial purpose of extremism.

CUCKOO TRICKS

Despite what the title of Oscar-winning film with Jack Nicholson[16] would suggest, cuckoos don't make nests. Instead, cuckoos lay their eggs into a nest built with great care by other birds. Love is blind, and the bird parents don't seem to notice an extra egg among theirs. When chicks hatch, the parent birds feed them all equally, cuckoos included. But evolution equipped cuckoos with one more trick. As the chick matures, it squeezes the other chicks out of the nest one by one, until the cuckoo is the only hatchling left. The parent birds, none the wiser, continue feeding the growing bird that killed their own offspring and took advantage of their enormous efforts to build a home and raise a family. Cuckoos are parasites that take advantage of the infrastructure and efforts of love.

Love abused. In some ways, radical groups and movements, religious cults, terrorist groups, authoritarian regimes, are like cuckoos. They take advantage of human mental infrastructure that evolved for love, extremist tendencies, protective aggression, and all. The narratives they use to recruit and indoctrinate followers squeeze out one's own loved ones—family, friends, even oneself—redirecting love toward the radical group and hate toward its targets. Cults and authoritarian regimes often make "squeezing out" of one's kin a rite of passage required to be accepted as a good citizen. In Stalin's USSR as in Mao's China, people were expected to snitch on their loved ones, and even to go along with clear fabrications of their loved ones' wrongdoings, becoming an instrument in state oppression against family and friends. In religious cults, people are often required to give up their spouses and children in the name of the cult.[17] This cuckoo pattern can also be found closer to home: a corporation demanding complete devotion, grueling hours and self-denial because "we are a family"; a college fraternity requiring deadly self-abuse from pledges desiring to become "brothers" use the same cuckoo bait and switch.

And because extremism is rooted in love, it is not surprising that people who are feeling lonely because they are rejected or bullied, or because they are different, or because they are away from home are especially susceptible to it. For us humans, love is essential, and we are ready to die and kill for it. When lacking love, we become easy marks for those who would abuse this need.

Leonard Cohen, a Canadian poet and a singer-songwriter, said it well. "We are not mad. We are human. We want to love, and someone must forgive us for the paths we take to love, for the paths are many and dark, and we are ardent and cruel in our journey."[18]

The Buddha's enlightenment began with his realization of some *noble truths* about the nature of human existence. The first was that suffering exists. The second that attachment is the root of suffering. As humans, we are bound by our nature: to love, to become attached to people, places, ideas, and to be extreme about it, to give it our all, to sacrifice and to fight for it. Humans love; love inspires extremism; extremism takes a toll. It's the circle of life, the Wheel of Samsara. The Buddha also had envisioned a way out of suffering. It and other useful suggestions for reducing the toll of extremism are examined in the chapters that follow.

IN SUMMARY

Love, this most profound human emotion, is readily capable of driving people to extremes. Because of its essential role in cementing a lasting bond within a couple, in turn so vital for child-rearing in the human species, love often becomes an overriding concern that overshadows all else; it often then elicits acts of sacrifice and recklessness that may appear foolish and irrational to outsiders. Whereas love's extremes are particularly apparent in instances of romantic love, they are pervasively present in love's other types, like motherly love, or love one feels for members of one's group, conceived of as an extended family, protection which may prompt one to risk life and limb, to kill and die. In its capacity to be driven to extremes, love is truly an emotion that "makes the world turn 'round" to build and also to destroy when love of own translates into hate of other.

NOTES

1 Burke, M. (2023, December 11). A royal crisis: The shocking moment king Edward viii announced his abdication to the nation. *BBC News.* https://www.bbc.com/culture/article/20231208-a-royal-crisis-the-shocking-moment-king-edward-viii-announced-his-abdication-to-the-nation

2 My Geo. (2023). *The legend of Niko Pirosmani.* https://mygeotrip.com/legend-niko-pirosmani

3 M. B. (n.d.). *РОБЕРТ ЛУИС СТИВЕНСОН (ЖИЗНЬ И ТВОРЧЕСТВО).* Philology. http://www.philology.ru/literature3/urnov-67.htm

4 Burkett, J. P., & Young, L. J. (2012). The behavioral, anatomical and pharmacological parallels between social attachment, love and addiction. *Psychopharmacology,* 224, 1–26. https://doi.org/10.1007/s00213-012-2794-x

5 Burkett, J. P., & Young, L. J. (2012). The behavioral, anatomical and pharmacological parallels between social attachment, love and addiction. *Psychopharmacology,* 224, 7. https://doi.org/10.1007/s00213-012-2794-x

6 Buss D. M. (1989). Sex differences in human mate preferences: Evolutionary hypotheses testing in 37 cultures. *Behavioral and Brain Sciences,* 12(1), 1–49. https://doi.org/10.1017/S0140525X00023992

7 Fisher, H. E., Aron, A., & Brown, L. L. (2006). Romantic love: A mammalian brain system for mate choice. *Philosophical Transactions of the Royal Society B: Biological Sciences,* 361(1476), 2173–2186. https://doi.org/10.1098/rstb.2006.1938

8 Buss, D. M. (1988). Love acts: The evolutionary biology of love. In R. J. Sternberg & M. L. Barnes (Eds.), *The psychology of love* (pp. 100–118). Yale University Press.

9 Bode, A., & Kushnick, G. (2021). Proximate and ultimate perspectives on romantic love. *Frontiers in Psychology,* 12, 573123. 10.3389/fpsyg.2021.573123

10 Gammie, S. C., & Lonstein, J. S. (2006). Maternal aggression. In Nelson R. J. (Ed.), *Biology of aggression* (pp. 250–274). Oxford University Press.

11 Hahn-Holbrook, J., Holbrook, C., & Haselton, M. G. (2011). Parental precaution: Neurobiological means and adaptive ends. *Neuroscience & Biobehavioral Reviews*, 35(4), 1052–1066. https://doi.org/10.1016/j.neubiorev.2010.09.015

12 Stein, A. (2021). *Terror, love and brainwashing: Attachment in cults and totalitarian systems*. Routledge.

13 Stein, A. (2021). *Terror, love and brainwashing: Attachment in cults and totalitarian systems*. Routledge.

14 Kruglanski, A. W., Bélanger, J. J., Gelfand, M., Gunaratna, R., Hettiarachchi, M., Reinares, F., ... Sharvit, K. (2013). Terrorism—A (self) love story: Redirecting the significance quest can end violence. *American Psychologist*, 68(7), 559. https://doi.org/10.1037/a0032615

15 Moskalenko, S., & Romanova, E. (2022). Deadly disinformation: Viral conspiracy theories as a radicalization mechanism. *The Journal of Intelligence, Conflict, and Warfare*, 5(2), 129–153. https://doi.org/10.21810/jicw.v5i2.5032

16 Wikimedia Foundation. (2024, July 16). One flew over the cuckoo's nest (film). *Wikipedia*. https://en.wikipedia.org/wiki/One_Flew_Over_the_Cuckoo%27s_Nest_(film)

17 Stein, A. (2021). *Terror, love and brainwashing: Attachment in cults and totalitarian systems*. Routledge.

18 Cohen, L. (2011). *Poems and stories: Cohen*. Penguin.

9

LITTLE THINGS THAT COUNT

It's easy to be impressed by famous extremists. So much struggle, so much fame! Extremism looms large because it is: salient, grand, memorable. In our time of social media-inspired social comparisons, and endless stories about extreme others who made it big, the inclination to emulate their feats is natural. But extremism's grandiosity obscures several important things. This chapter is about what stays in extremism's shadow.

THE COST

In previous chapters, we have differentiated socially destructive extremism that spreads waves of suffering—such as terrorism, fascism or crime—from socially constructive extremism that promotes social advancement and cultural evolution—through scientific, artistic or humanistic pursuits. It's easy to conclude that as long as one follows a socially constructive extremist path, one should reap nothing but rewards.

It ain't necessarily so.

In fact, extremism of any kind is harmful to the extremists themselves. The single-minded pursuit of a passion for which one gives up food and sleep, social connections, and fulfillment of alternative needs takes its toll. One's physical health might deteriorate as it did for Maria Sklodowska-Curie because of her work with radioactive

DOI: 10.4324/9781003472476-9

materials. One's mental health may decline as it did for Van Gogh, who suffered from deep depression. Social life is likely to wither, as friends, colleagues, and even family fade away given the extremist's overriding focus on their singular supreme goal. Unless the extremism is about one's work, professional life too may deteriorate as a result of the extremist's neglect of their work duties. Political extremism, even the constructive kind, tends to shorten one's life expectancy, as activists stand out not just to those who admire their extremism but also to those who abhor it. Both Gandhi and Martin Luther King, Jr., were killed for their activism; countless others were jailed and tortured for their zealous devotion to their cause. Even extremism of maternal love, the ultimate, life-giving kind of extremism, exerts a heavy toll on the woman's body that significantly ages it. Research on telomeres,[1] tiny particles of DNA that reflect the body's age, found that women who had given live births had telomeres 4.2% shorter than their counterparts with no children. This is equivalent to 11 years of accelerated cellular aging. All those sleepless nights and days of worry, all that self-sacrifice that caring for a child entails chips away at women's health and wellbeing. The costs of extremism, indeed, are varied and high.

Sometimes, extremism is not a choice but a necessity, the only way to survive. Being in a desert with nothing to drink forces one to devote every last bit of energy to finding water. A mental illness or a substance addiction hijacks one's ability to make non-extreme choices. When a child is bullied at school, abused, or made into a soldier, they respond the only way they can stay alive, and that way is often extreme. At other times, extremism is inspired in capable adults by stories, movies, or examples suggesting that the only way to get ahead is the extreme way. Inspirational quotes framed on office walls, blockbuster movies, and pep talks of coaches and teachers—all seem to suggest that the sole road to success is through self-sacrifice, agony, torment, and pain, in the words of Mother Theresa who led a life of self-denial, helping Calcutta's poor, (any worthwhile achievement) "must cost, must hurt, must [demand that we] empty ourselves."

But is that really true? In focusing exclusively on extremists' achievements, we glorify extremism, losing sight of its downsides, and of the possibilities that moderation offers. Often, human errors are caused by exclusive attention to one side of the coin while ignoring the other as the following true story illustrates.

SURVIVORSHIP BIAS[2]

During World War II, the US military faced the considerable challenge of reducing costly aircraft casualties. The experts examined the damage to the planes that returned from combat, and aggregated the results. The aircraft wings and tail clearly showed more bullet holes, whereas the engine remained mostly intact. The US military's experts concluded that the wings and tails had to be reinforced, since they were clearly more vulnerable. However, Abraham Wald, a statistician and methodologist, offered a completely opposite solution: to reinforce the engine, leaving the wings and tails as is. His idea, now known as survivorship bias, was that the US military was only looking at the planes that survived an attack, and forgetting about those that perished. The survived planes' damage was non-lethal; if anything, it showed the planes' ability to sustain this kind of damage and still return to their home base. On the other hand, the planes that did not make it back were far more likely to have had bullets reach their engines. Armoring the engine, therefore, was the best measure against aircraft casualties.

Survivorship bias is widespread because we tend to look at salient examples of something, ignoring the (often more numerous) cases that remain out of view. Boys who want to play for the NBA are inspired by NBA players, who are famous and rich, and have shoes named after them. The aspiring basketball stars think that putting all their efforts into basketball, practicing day and night, neglecting school and other activities, will bring them the success of Michael Jordan or LeBron James. What their survivorship bias overlooks are the untold numbers of boys who bet all their time and effort on basketball—only to be neglected by scouts, suffer an injury, or simply not grow tall enough—and end up missing important opportunities. Girls who want to be ballerinas have a similar survivorship bias when investing all their time in ballet practice in the hope of becoming prima ballerinas, despite the odds that make it far more likely they develop an eating disorder.[3]

Great success stories that contain elements of extremism catch people's attention precisely because they depart from the ordinary and prosaic ways of doing things. In their glamour and grandeur, they conceal many other instances, where extreme pursuit extracted all the costs but yielded none of the benefits, or where the success came from boring, grinding work day after tedious day. Before embarking on an extreme pursuit in the hope of attaining outstanding success, it is good to take into account survivorship bias, and devote resources according to the odds of success, and its likely costs.

ALTERNATIVES

Moderation. It is perhaps ironic that, although religions can inspire assorted extremisms, from holy wars to monastery life, they are often based on teachings of moderation. Jesus told his followers to "give to Caesar what's Caesar's and to God what's God's;" he allowed his disciples to pick wheat on Saturday (contrary to Jewish religious prohibition from doing work on Sabbath); and he was criticized by his detractors for his less than extreme lifestyle, "The Son of Man has come eating and drinking, and you say, 'Look at him! A glutton and a drunkard, a friend of tax collectors and sinners!'"[4]

Judaism, too, recommends moderation, as summarized by a 12th century influential Jewish thinker Maimonides, "To avoid lust or envy, do not say I won't eat good food, or marry. This is an evil way... One who follows that path is a sinner"[5]. Maimonides recommended the pursuit of a middle path in which one is "neither... easily angered" nor, like the dead, "does not feel."[6]

In Islam, *wasat* (moderation) is one of the most central characteristics of the creed. Wasat refers to a balanced life, avoiding extremes and experiencing things in moderation:[7] "And upon Allah is the direction of the [right/moderate/straight] way, and among the various paths are those deviating. And if He willed, He could have guided you all."[8]

Siddhartha Gautama, later known as the Buddha, famously experienced both extreme indulgence, as a rich prince protected from even the sight of suffering by palace walls, and extreme self-denial as a wandering ascetic deprived of food, shelter, and comfort. Becoming enlightened, the Buddha realized the source of suffering and the way out of it. Buddhism is based on what he called "the middle way,"[9] a path of moderation where both one's body and one's soul merit attention, and neither should be neglected in service of the other.

Very well, you might say, but what if I want to accomplish great things—wouldn't moderation hold me back? Wouldn't I fall behind more extreme individuals? Not necessarily. Sometimes, moderation is by far the winning strategy.

Ancient Greek fabulist Aesop told a parable of a race between a hare and a tortoise:[10] the hare dashed ahead but then got tired and took a nap; the tortoise, moving at its moderate pace, eventually passed him by. Slow and steady won the race. On the other side of the world, Chinese philosopher Confucius succinctly agreed: "It does not matter how slowly you go as long as you don't stop." Spinning the globe one more time we find yet another confirmation that moderation can achieve success where extremism fails—this story is from the South Pole.

Before 1911, every expedition that attempted to reach the South Pole ended in tragic failure. The deadly cold, hazardous terrain, and unpredictable weather claimed the lives of numerous courageous explorers. It was with the knowledge of these failed attempts of their predecessors that a Norwegian, Roald Amundsen, and an Englishman, Robert Falcon Scott, embarked on their respective missions, in a race to be the first to reach the South Pole. Each had a unique approach: Scott drove his team to the extreme during favorable weather, covering as much distance as possible, and hunkered down in their tents during adverse conditions. In contrast, Amundsen was determined to maintain a moderate daily pace of 15 miles, regardless of the weather.

By December 12, 1911, Amundsen and his team were just 45 miles from the South Pole. "Going and surface as good as ever," Amundsen wrote in his journal. "Weather splendid—calm with sunshine." Despite his estimation of the weather being splendid and surface good, which would allow the team to reach the Pole that day (remember, they were in a race, and had no idea how far the other team was), Amundsen adhered to his strategy of not exceeding the daily 15-mile limit. Amundsen's team, true to his moderate pace, arrived at the Pole two days later, on December 14.

What about team extreme? Scott's team reached the Pole 34 days after Amundsen's team. They were greeted by the flying Norwegian flag that signified their defeat—they failed to be the first to reach the South Pole. On the return journey, Scott insisted on maintaining the "inhuman exertion" during good weather. This led to severe frostbites and exhaustion, which tragically resulted in Scott and his entire team freezing to death. Meanwhile, Amundsen's crew, sticking to their 15-miles-per-day pace, completed the 1400-mile journey back without any issues.[11] Pacing oneself can be a life-saving measure, as well as a recipe for success.

Behavioral science research supports this idea. Behavior change is difficult to achieve, and even more difficult to maintain. The struggle is real for anyone who has ever tried to lose weight, exercise more, or use social media less. In the short term, dramatic interventions such as extreme dieting or going "cold turkey" can yield results. But over time, the gains achieved through extremism tend to dissipate, and the old behavior returns, erasing the gains. A better strategy is habit formation.[12,13] Habit formation consists of making small changes in daily routine that have a good chance of turning into habits. Good habits, in turn, are more likely to lead to lasting positive results— even if they take longer to attain.

Researchers provided a helpful tool for people who wish to adopt this empirically validated strategy.[14] It is geared to health-oriented behaviors, but can easily be used for other goals. Studies demonstrated that, when implemented consistently, *by week* 10 the new behavior typically feels a lot more automatic (and therefore less effortful), and it actually becomes "quite strange" to not do it. The positive effects of the behavioral change should also be observed at that time.

Make a new healthy habit

1. Decide on a goal that you would like to achieve for your health.
2. Choose a simple action that will get you toward your goal which you can do on a daily basis.
3. Plan when and where you will do your chosen action. Be consistent: choose a time and place that you encounter every day of the week.
4. Every time you encounter that time and place, do the action.
5. It will get easier with time, and within 10 weeks you should find you are doing it automatically without even having to think about it.
6. Congratulations, you've made a healthy habit!

My goal (e.g. "to eat more fruit and vegetables")

_____

My plan (e.g. "after I have lunch at home I will have a piece of fruit")
(When   and   where)   _____   I
will _____

Some people find it helpful to keep a record while they are forming a new habit. This daily tick-sheet can be used until your new habit becomes automatic. You can rate how automatic it feels at the end of each week, to watch it getting easier.

	Week 1	Week 2	Week 3	Week 4	Week 5	Week 6	Week 7	Week 8	Week 9	Week 10
Monday										
Tuesday										
Wednesday										
Thursday										
Friday										
Saturday										
Sunday										
Done on >5 days, yes or no										
How automatic does it feel? Rate from 1 (not at all) to 10 (completely)										

The Nobel Prize-winning author, Ernest Hemingway, arrived at a similar wisdom of moderation by trial and error. His practice of writing between 1,000 and 2,000 words a day, working from 2AM until dawn, left Hemingway feeling "the real old melancholia." He discovered that "it is better to produce half as much, get plenty of exercise and not go crazy."[15] Hemingway's hard-won, timeless advise to writers is to aim for a moderate goal of 500 words a day (two pages typed, double spaced), but with the caveat of doing it consistently.

"Nothing great in the world has ever been accomplished without passion," said the great German philosopher Georg Wilhelm Friedrich Hegel.[16] However, passion need not be equal to extremism. In this realm, Canadian psychologist Robert Vallerand aptly distinguished between *harmonious* and *obsessive* types of passion.[17] Whereas obsessive passion is extreme denoting as it does an exclusive focus on its object to the total neglect of other needs, harmonious passion apportions one's time between the needs sequentially, devoting all of one's resources to one's overriding interest at appointed times, yet at other times attending to all one's other concerns, affording a healthier, more balanced life.

In achieving any goal, be it a healthy lifestyle or good writing, slow but consistent progress is often superior to spurts of extremism that can make one feel on top of the world, but leave exhaustion and lack of motivation in their wake. "The middle way" sometimes affords a more reliable pathway to success.

KINDNESS

We have discussed the ways in which extremism separates the person engaged in it from their social network: family, friends, co-workers. It is not only through spending all their time and effort in their preferred activity that extremists' isolation grows (or they gravitate toward other extremists), but also because they tend to disregard social norms and the feelings of people who try to maintain a relationship with them. Extremists like Steve Jobs can be arrogant and brash; others, like Incels, can be socially awkward, or, like the South

Pole explorer Robert Scott, too wrapped up in their own ambition to worry about the wellbeing of others. Extremists can be too hard on people around them, demanding they adhere to their own dietary and lifestyle restrictions, as did Gandhi, or indeed they can sacrifice others' lives to advance their radical agenda, as did Osama bin Laden. Our next suggestion aims not to reduce extremism directly, but rather to mitigate its negative effects on people affected by it. The suggestion is, simply, to be kind.

Major religions recommend paying attention to fellow humans, and practicing kindness. "Love thy neighbor as yourself," and "do unto others as you have them do unto you" were Jesus' instructions to his followers. In Judaism, Hillel the Elder (110 BC) summarized the gist of the Jewish faith through the *Golden Rule*, "What is hateful to you, do not do to your neighbor: this is the whole Torah; the rest is explanation."[18] In Islam, Prophet Mohammed instructed followers to "Help your brother, whether he is an oppressor or an oppressed one."[19] The Buddha discovered an eight-fold path to help avoid suffering, which included three elements specifically concerned with not causing harm.[20] These are *right speech*: avoiding saying things that would hurt or harm others; *right action*: ensuring that our physical actions do not cause harm to either others or ourselves; *right livelihood*: avoiding livelihoods that cause suffering in others by cheating, harming, or killing them. A Buddhist teacher and author, Pema Chodron, summarized, "The most straightforward advice on awakening enlightened mind is this: practice not causing harm to anyone—yourself or others—and every day, do what you can to be helpful."[21]

As we described in Chapter 8, extremism often stems from human need to love and be loved. Its primordial function is to promote pair bonding and child-rearing. Even the socially destructive kind of extremism, such as terrorism, is usually a form of defensive aggression against those who are perceived as harming or threatening a cherished person, group, or idea. And often extremism arises from a history of personal or social rejection: bullying, abuse, isolation, or discrimination. Kindness can help reduce extremism by addressing its underlying need.

Recall our story about Don Ritchie, an Australian whose house looked onto a tall cliff from which people like to jump to their deaths. Over about 50 years, Ritchie saved at least 180 would-be jumpers (according to his family the number is closer to 500)—by watching the cliff, rushing over when he saw a person standing over it, and inviting them to his house for a cup of tea. Individuals who drove up to the cliff were in the grip of extremism, ready to throw their lives away. With only a tiny kindness—an offer of tea and time—Ritchie was able to divert them from their destructive path.

Acts of kindness can originate not only from individuals but also from groups. In 2011, the Arab Spring ignited a revolution against Egypt's president Hosni Mubarak. During this period of unrest and frequent violent crashes between the protestors and the state security forces, Christian protesters in Cairo's Tahrir Square formed a human wall by linking hands to protect a group of praying Muslims.

In Egypt, Christians are often targeted by Islamic extremist groups and frequently lack protection from the police and military, making large gatherings like Mass particularly vulnerable. But a few days after the kindness that the Christian protestors showed their Muslim compatriots, Muslims reciprocated this act of solidarity.[22] During a Mass in Cairo's central plaza, Muslims in traditional attire linked hands to shield the praying Christians from potential violence. After the service, the combined crowd of Muslims and Christians chanted "one hand," celebrating their unity while holding up both Qurans and crosses. Even with a longstanding history of violent extremism between the two groups, an act of kindness can be appreciated and reciprocated, and as a result, extremism on both sides can be reduced.

This, precisely, is the rationale behind I Am Your Protector,[23] a group that seeks to reduce extremism and hate through the sharing of inspirational stories about people who protected others, typically members of victimized outgroups, from harm often through acts of heroism and self-endangerment. I Am Your Protector was founded single-handedly by Andrea (Dani) Varadi, herself a political refugee, and stateless until the age of 13. The credo of IAYP is based on the observation that the media has a strong negativity bias and predominantly reports on instances of hatred, polarization, and fear. To correct this imbalance, IAYP collects and disseminates countless tales of people who stand up for one another, thus promoting the sense of unity and fellowship between groups that have seen themselves as bitter antagonists of each other.

One such story, dating back to World War II, is that of Khaled Abdul-Wahab, who in December 1942 ferried two dozen Jews from the town of Mahdia on the Easter shore of Tunisia, thus saving them from the occupying German troops. Khaled hid his "guests" in his estate, 20 miles away from Mahdia till May 1943 when they were able to depart safely after the British Seventh Armored Division captured Tunis, the capital of Tunisia, and the US II Army Corps captured Bizerte, the last remaining port in the Axis hands.

A more recent story of a protector is that of Hesham Ahmad Mohammad, a 32-year-old primary school teacher from Aleppo, who in 2016 was celebrating New Year's Eve with other Syrian friends in Cologne, Germany, when they rescued a young American woman from sexual assault by forming a protective cordon around her to help escape a violent crowd.

The IAYP disseminates these and numerous other stories as model tales that highlight the values of human fellowship and compassion often across group boundaries and partitions that promote hate, callousness, and brutality toward fellow human beings.

Psychology research supports this tampering effect of kindness on extremism. In a study of Americans with radically opposite political views, staunch Republicans or Democrats, greater empathy toward the other group, whether it was dispositional (the person was naturally inclined to be kind) or experimentally induced (the person was encouraged by the researchers to feel greater kindness), predicted lower polarization of opinions, and lower animosity toward the opposite group.[24] Research consistently found that communication across conflict-ridden group boundaries that conveys interpersonal warmth and kindness is far more likely to foster cooperation and reduce hostility than communication that does not convey these sentiments.[25]

In one cutting-edge study, researchers designed a phone app, called Random App of Kindness, which engaged users (children and teens) in empathy-building practices in the form of games. These included recognizing emotions in others, caring for a crying baby, petting a dog, etc. After using the app for two months (compared to control group that used a different app), participants were significantly more likely to feel compassion for someone in need and to behave in empathetic ways when interacting with a stranger; they were also less likely to endorse physical violence and less likely to behave aggressively toward peers.[26]

As helpful as kindness can be to others, it is also important to be kind to oneself. In mindfulness training, participants are sometimes asked to reflect on whether they would use the type of talk or expectations they reserve for themselves with their best friend, their child, or a loved one. Often, we are our harshest critics, cruel, merciless, and unreasonable. If we would never say "stupid" or "well here you go AGAIN" to our children when they make a mistake, if we would never expect our best friend to forgo needed rest or comfort, we deserve the same consideration. Being kind to self and others is likely to not only reduce extremism, but also to foster a more rewarding life.

DILIGENCE

A Native American fable speaks of a hummingbird named Dukdukdiya. One day, a fierce fire engulfed Dukdukdiya's native forest. As other animals great and small ran for their lives, or froze in petrified stupor, the hummingbird alone took action. Time and time again, Dukdukdiya carried a single drop of water in her beak from a nearby stream to the forest, dropping it onto the flames, then going back for more. Finally, the bear, the biggest of all animals in the forest, asked the hummingbird what it hoped to accomplish with its one drop of water against a fire as great as this. "Without stopping, Dukdukdiya looked down at all of the animals. She said, 'I am doing what I can.'"[27] The story says the tiny hummingbird's actions so touched the gods that they then sent a rainstorm to fall over the forest and quench the fire.

Sometimes, overwhelming threats make it seem that only extremism can make any difference. The result of this perception, the fable above described, is that most people end up doing nothing, overwhelmed by the odds against them. But there is an alternative: to do what one can.

In February 2022, Russian Federation—the world's largest country with a population of 140 million, unlimited oil and gas revenue, nuclear weapons, navy, and mandatory military conscription attacked Ukraine—population 40 million, no nukes (that it once had and gave up by signing the 1994 Budapest memorandum), no navy, and no military conscription. With these odds, Russia, as well as many other nations' military analysts, believed that Ukraine will fall within days. And at first, it seemed highly likely. But then something incredible happened.

Ordinary Ukrainians, civilians without weapons or hope to prevail against tanks and supersonic missiles, did "what they could," like the hummingbird carrying a drop of water to the raging fire. A woman downed a Russian drone with a jar of pickled tomatoes she threw at it from her balcony.[28] A man stole a Russian tank and turned it over to the Ukrainian military.[29] Unarmed villagers blocked roads with their bodies, standing in front of Russian tanks and BMPs and chanting for them to go home.[30] In city bomb shelters, people knit camouflage nets for soldiers on the front lines. Volunteers organized collection of money and purchase of everything from first aid kits to bulletproof vests and evacuation vehicles. Every day, the social media supplied new stories of ordinary Ukrainians doing what they could, and drop by drop by drop, this turned the course of the war around.

The determination of ordinary Ukrainians to stand up to a force much greater than theirs convinced foreign leaders to support Ukraine in the war against Russia and to provide much-needed military assistance. Not only state officials, but ordinary citizens around the world donated money to the Ukrainian cause; they opened their homes to Ukrainian refugees and participated in mass demonstrations in support of Ukraine. Some even traveled to Ukraine to fight in the war. And so it was, against the odds, that little Ukraine resisted what was hailed as the second mightiest military in the world, thanks in large part to people doing what they could, even if it was but a drop.

Recent American history also offers examples of ordinary people doing what they can, and it making a huge difference. The Catholic Church sex abuse scandal only became public, and the Church was made to pay for its violations, because a group of dedicated journalists did their job. Similarly, the death of George Floyd, which became a rallying cry for protests against police brutality around the USA, was only able to effect that political movement because one young woman recorded the tragedy on her cell phone and shared it with the world. The journalists, the witness who filmed the murder of Floyd and shared the video did what they could: exposing the crime and cruelty of a much larger and more powerful entity.

The issues that inspire extremism can be of planetary magnitude. Climate change, for example, is so daunting that its threat increasingly causes mental health issues among young people, called climate anxiety.[31] We may feel helpless against something so big. And these feelings of helplessness can inspire extremism, both in those who wish to stop it and in those who wish to deny it's happening.[32] But there is an alternative to both helpless passivity and extremist action, and that is doing what we can, even if it seems like a drop. Reducing the use of plastics and synthetics, reusing and recycling, eating less red meat—it is not much, but it is something we can do. As American writer and Unitarian cleric Edward Everett Hale said, "I am only one, but I am one. I cannot do everything, but I can do something. And I will not let what I cannot do interfere with what I can do."

Moderation, kindness, and diligence are not as glamorous as extremism, but then they save us from the vast costs that extremism often exacts. While perhaps less likely to bring fame and glory they are more likely to result in harmony and peace. And with everyone trying for team extreme these days, who knows—maybe a better way to make a difference is to pace yourself, be kind to self and others, and do what one can even if it is not much.

IN SUMMARY

Because it stands out and departs from the mundane, extremism catches people's attention and sticks in people's memory. Particularly when extremists can claim notable achievements, their radical ways may be emulated by numerous wannabes blinded by the extremists' fame to the dark side of the coin: the toll in physical and mental health that extremism typically exacts. The disproportionate focus on extremists' impact also beclouds achievements begotten through harmonious moderation, and the quiet contentment that balanced life affords, hailed by gurus throughout the ages as a way of "the Golden Mean."

NOTES

1 Bhanoo, S. (2019, October 19). Do pregnancy and childbirth age women on a cellular level? maybe—The Washington Post. *The Washington Post*. https:// www.washingtonpost.com/health/do-pregnancy-and-childbirth-acceler- ate-aging-in-women-maybe/2019/10/18/635dbd7c-e516-11e9-b403 -f738899982d2_story.html

2 Thomas, J. (2019, July 8). Bullet holes & bias: The story of Abraham Wald— mcdreeamie-Musings. *Mcdreeamie*. https://mcdreeamiemusings.com/blog /2019/4/1/survivorship-bias-how-lessons-from-world-war-two-affect -clinical-research-today

3 Arcelus, J., Witcomb, G. L., & Mitchell, A. (2014). Prevalence of eating dis- orders amongst dancers: A systemic review and meta-analysis. *European Eating Disorders Review*, 22(2), 92–101. https://doi.org/10.1002/erv.2271

4 Bible Gateway. (n.d.). *Bible gateway passage: Luke 7:34—English standard version*. https://www.biblegateway.com/passage/?search=Luke+7%3A34&ver- sion=ESV

5 (Mishneh Torah, Laws of Character Development and Ethical Ideas 3:1)

6 Mencher, E. H. (n.d.-a). *Everything in moderation...except moderation*. Reform Judaism. https://reformjudaism.org/everything-moderationexcept -moderation

7 Kamali, M. H. (2015). *The middle path of moderation in Islam: The Qur'ānic principle of wasaṭiyyah*. Oxford University Press.

8 *Surah An-Nahl 16:1–9—towards understanding the Quran*. Quran, Hadith & Literature. (n.d.). https://www.islamicstudies.info/tafheem.php?sura=16

9   *The Middle Way.* (2022, September 26). Soka Gakkai (global). https://www
    .sokaglobal.org/resources/study-materials/buddhist-concepts/the-mid-
    dle-way.html#:~:text=In%20the%20broadest%20sense%2C%20the,chal-
    lenges%20of%20life%20and%20society.

10 *The hare & the tortoise.* Library of Congress Aesop Fables. (n.d.). https://read
    .gov/aesop/025.html

11 Oppenheimer, B. (2024, May 20). SIX at 6: Diverting a meteor, one caveat,
    the last place on Earth, losing 140 pounds, career trajectories, and sailing
    to the horizon. *Billy Oppenheimer.* https://billyoppenheimer.com/may-19
    -2024/

12 Gardner, B., Lally, P., & Wardle, J. (2012). Making health habitual: The psy-
    chology of "habit-formation" and general practice. *British Journal of General
    Practice*, 62(605), 664–666. https://doi.org/10.3399/bjgp12X659466

13 Wood, W. (2019). *Good habits, bad habits: The science of making positive changes that
    stick.* Picador.

14 Gardner, B., Lally, P., & Wardle, J. (2012). Making health habitual: The psy-
    chology of "habit-formation" and general practice. *British Journal of General
    Practice*, 62(605), 664–666. https://doi.org/10.3399/bjgp12X659466

15 Firth, K. (2017, March 17). Hemingway's advice to writers. *Research Degree
    Insiders.*   https://researchinsiders.blog/2017/03/17/hemingways-advice
    -to-writers/

16 Appleton Creative. (2018, October 23). Nothing great in the world has ever
    been accomplished without passion. *Pinterest.* https://tr.pinterest.com/pin
    /158400111879196363/#:~:text=%22Nothing%20great%20in%20the
    %20world,Friedrich%20Hegel%20%23goals%20%23inspi%E2%80%A6
    &text=Inspirational%20quotes%2C%20Accomplishment%2C%20Hegel

17 Vallerand, R. J. (2015). *The psychology of passion: A dualistic model.* Oxford
    University Press.

18 Wikimedia Foundation. (2024b, July 18). *Golden rule.* Wikipedia. https://en
    .wikipedia.org/wiki/Golden_Rule#:~:text=What%20is%20hateful%20to
    %20you,the%20explanation%3B%20go%20and%20learn.&text=Hillel
·   %20recognized%20brotherly%20love%20as%20the%20fundamental%2
    0principle%20of%20Jewish%20ethics. Sahih al-Bukhari 2444 Book 46,
    Hadith 5.

19 *Sahih al-Bukhari 2444 Book 46, Hadith 5: Oppressions.* Sunnah. (n.d.). https://sun-
    nah.com/bukhari:2444

20 Namchak. (2024, April 8). *Noble eightfold path: Namchak community: Tibetan
    Buddhism.* Namchak Tibetan Buddhist Practice & Retreat. https://www
    .namchak.org/community/blog/the-noble-eightfold-path/?utm_source

=adwords&utm_medium=ppc&utm_campaign=Advanced%2BBuddhism
&utm_term=buddha+8+fold+path&hsa_tgt=kwd-299403302558&hsa_
grp=124337158023&hsa_cam=1534618725&hsa_net=adwords&hsa_src
=g&hsa_mt=b&hsa_acc=8734074612&hsa_kw=buddha+8+fold+path
&hsa_ver=3&hsa_ad=538403321969&gad_source=1&gclid=Cj0KCQjwj
9-zBhDyARIsAERjds3R4UtYEkpVaVb1VT7KKdzY2qZEpPt81VkUF6e6
OYr6DAzgLTouXflaAt-lEALw_wcB

21 Sangha. (2015, February 14). *What to do when the going gets rough.* Buddhist
Sangha of Bucks County. https://buddhistsangha.com/2015/02/13/what
-to-do-when-the-going-gets-rough/

22 Alexander, A. (2011, February 10). Egypt's Muslims and Christians join
hands in protest. *BBC News.* https://www.bbc.com/news/world-middle
-east-12407793

23 *Home.* (2024, March 20). I Am Your Protector. https://iamyourprotector
.org/

24 Santos, L. A., Voelkel, J. G., Willer, R., & Zaki, J. (2022). Belief in the utility
of cross-partisan empathy reduces partisan animosity and facilitates political persuasion. *Psychological Science, 33*(9), 1557–1573. https://doi.org/10
.1177/09567976221098594

25 Andersen, S. M., Saribay, S. A., & Thorpe, J. S. (2008). Simple kindness
can go a long way: Relationships, social identity, and engagement. *Social
Psychology, 39*(1), 59–69. https://doi.org/10.1027/1864-9335.39.1.59

26 Konrath, S., Martingano, A. J., Tolman, R. M., Winslow, M., & Bushman, B.
J. (2023). Random app of kindness: Evaluating the potential of a smart-
phone intervention to impact adolescents' empathy, prosocial behavior, and
aggression. *Psychology of Popular Media,* 13(3), 338–352. https://doi.org/10
.1037/ppm0000478

27 Yahgulanaas, M. N. (2012). *Flight of the hummingbird: A parable for the environment*
(p. 30). Greystone Books.

28 Jankowicz, M. (2022, March 8). A grandma in Kyiv says she took out a
suspicious drone while Russia was attacking by throwing a jar of pickled tomatoes at it. *Business Insider.* https://www.businessinsider.com/kyiv
-grandma-took-down-ussian-drone-with-jar-tomato-pickles-2022-3

29 Chaturvedi, A. (2022, March 1). Ukrainian farmer "steals" Russian tank
using tractor, internet delighted. *NDTV.com.* https://www.ndtv.com/
world-news/ukrainian-farmer-steals-russian-tank-using-tractor-internet
-delighted-2796370

30 Eastham, J. (2022, February 27). "Together we are strong": Ukrainian civilians stop Russian tank from entering village. *The Telegraph*. https://www .telegraph.co.uk/world-news/2022/02/27/together-strong-ukrainian -civilians-stop-russian-tank-entering/

31 Dodds, J. (2021). The psychology of climate anxiety. *BJPsych Bulletin*, 45(4), 222–226. doi:10.1192/bjb.2021.18

32 Shanaah, S., Fritsche, I., & Osmundsen, M. (2024). Support for pro-climate and ecofascist extremism: Correlates and intersections. *Democracy and Security*, 20(1), 46–68. https://doi.org/10.1080/17419166.2023.2220111

10

INVITING EXTREMISM TO TEA

In our book's final chapter, we recoup the main features of extremism and outline ways in which extremism could be mitigated and nudged toward moderation.

RARITY

As we have emphasized throughout the book, there is more to extremism than what the mass media would suggest. Whereas their use of "extreme" typically refers to politically motivated violence, extremism is much broader and more diverse. It is true that violence is aptly described as extreme because it is relatively rare; most people most of the time aren't violent. The term "extreme" essentially expresses the behavior's infrequency, its statistical scarcity. This brings to mind a host of other behaviors that are rare and unusual, and hence extreme. The daily newspaper, the TV newscast, the internet and its various platforms are replete with narratives of extremism. Indeed, extremism is so interesting to people precisely because it is so rare and unusual.

A recent story in the *Washington Post* (6/21/2024) about Eric Holt, the aspiring runner, is one among many fascinating tales of extremism. Holt, 29, is bent on qualifying for the Olympics in the 1,500

DOI: 10.4324/9781003472476-10

meters event, despite hardships that would discourage most other people. He does not have a sponsor, so he pays for his own equipment, physiotherapist, and travel. For years he has been training by himself, often late at night after 13-hour shifts at a mental health clinic where he works as a ward. His meager salary can't cover both his athletic aspirations and the expenses of everyday living; therefore, he lives with his parents, and lets his girlfriend finance their outings. Yet he persists despite the obstacles. He hopes against hope that one day his luck will turn, and he will stand vindicated, and rewarded for his grit.

Like Holt, Alex Honnold, arguably the world's most accomplished climber who scaled "free solo" (i.e. without protective equipment) the formidable El Capitan peak in Yosemite Park, "dirtbagged" for years in a van as a social recluse with a single-minded focus on his passion. Countless other athletes also self-imposed long periods of self-denial for the sake of their ambitious quests. And in previous chapters we recounted stories about artists, scientists, humanitarians, and activists who carried out behaviors most people would balk at— attesting to these behaviors' rarity and extremism. Their stories are well known because they are so unique. As a result, they often make a splash in the news, and are then put up as models and admired.

SACRIFICE

There is another element beside rarity that characterizes extremism: self-sacrifice. The extremist's single-minded pursuit of their goals comes at a price. The physical and social deprivations can be painful and lonely, sometimes driving the extremist to despair, and causing mental issues including self-doubt, anxiety, and depression, as discussed in Chapter 6. The self-sacrifice that extremism demands is likely what largely accounts for its rarity: most people most of the time aren't willing to suffer as much. Why then, you might ask, are the extremists ready to do it? Are they irrational?

RATIONALITY

Social thinkers who studied the concept of rationality (the renowned sociologists Max Weber, and Emile Durkheim, and the Nobel Prize-winning psychologist Herbert Simon) defined it in terms of a match between one's goal and the means one selects for its attainment.[1] A means that is effective in reaching the goal is deemed rational, whereas a means that is ineffective or detrimental to a goal is deemed irrational. In the extreme state of mind, one goal dominates all others, and an activity that seems to serve it best is the rational choice. This is so even if the activity is inimical to alternative concerns, simply because, given the extremist's single-track mind, none of those concerns matter, as they are overridden by the focal, dominant purpose.

Consider, for instance, a suicide bomber ready to sacrifice their life on the altar of some cause. To those of us for whom life is important, their action makes no sense and therefore seems irrational. If living is the goal, killing oneself is senseless. Not for the bomber, however. Because for them, the end of attaining great significance in return of their self-sacrifice is more important than life itself.

And it is not only terrorists who value life less than their goal. "Give me freedom or give me death," famously exclaimed an American revolutionary Patrick Henry. "The unexamined life is not worth living," said Socrates. Extremists devalue everything, even life, relative to their goal.

THE PORTION MAKES THE POISON: HOW EXTREME IS "EXTREME"?

Extremism lies on a continuum defined by the degree to which a given need or concern is prioritized over others. When a concern is prioritized to merely a slight degree, one wouldn't talk of extremism, but rather of preference. The term "extremism" better fits a situation where the prioritization reaches a point at which the focal need is so dominant that it effectively makes one forget all else. In other words, motivational imbalance is a matter of degree, and only at its high degrees, where some of the individual's needs are sacrificed or neglected in favor of this one dominant concern, one may speak of extremism.

A question is then, "how extreme is extreme?" There is no simple answer. We can look at one's score on the extremism scale (Chapter 3), and if the score is high, conclude that the person is an extremist. But what if a person did not fill out the questionnaire? Counter-terrorism practitioners often recommend for family members or loved ones to be alert to the person's severing of social ties as a result of their singular focus. This behavior is a "red flag" that merits concern and possible intervention (especially when the person's singular focus is a violent extremist ideology or group). Finally, we can consider the way mental health professionals approach diagnostically distinguishing between a normal psychology and an abnormal one. The *Diagnostic and Statistical Manual* (DSM) takes into account symptom severity, duration, and functional impairment stemming from these. It's normal to be anxious or sad sometimes, but when one's mood interferes with one's social or professional life and causes persistent suffering, it is considered disordered. Similarly, it's normal to be impassioned at times, but when it takes over one's life and interferes with day-to-day functioning, causing suffering to self or others, it probably merits the term "extremism."

EXTREMISM AND YOU

We all have a capacity for motivational imbalance, and we often momentarily prioritize one need over others. In times of emergency, we "drop everything" to attend to the life and death issue—a fire, a sick child, a terror attack. These situations would elicit extreme behavior from almost anyone.

A 1982 film *Sophie's Choice* tells the tragic story of a Polish immigrant to the USA, Sophie Zawistowska (played by Meryl Streep), who during World War II was sent to Auschwitz with her two children, a son Jan and a daughter Ewa. Upon arrival at the camp, she had been forced to choose which one of her children would be sent to the gas chamber and killed, and in case of her refusal to choose, both would be killed. Desperately, she chose to send her daughter Eva to the gas chamber in order to save her son Jan.

This heart-wrenching story exemplifies a situation in which extremism is virtually inescapable. Sacrificing one's child is certainly an extreme act, yet Sophie was compelled to do it in violation of her maternal feelings. Guilt-ridden for the rest of her life, she ultimately committed suicide.

We might feel empathy for Sophie and see ourselves behaving similarly in her horrific circumstances. We are less likely to identify with other extremists: with zealots willing to kill and be killed for some cause, or with "mad scientists" pursuing their special idée fixe with abandon. Simply, we cannot envisage ourselves in their shoes. But the last century of social psychology has taught us that situations can be extremely powerful in eliciting the same behavior from most people. Should we find ourselves in extreme circumstances, we too might have done things we presently cannot imagine doing.

Some situations are readily identified as an emergency (e.g. fires, road accidents, tsunamis). Other situations are defined as such by trusted others. For example, ideologues and influencers may convince their followers that a given circumstance is dire and calls for an urgent reaction. Recruiters for Islamist terrorist organizations, Al Qaeda and ISIS, have been known to persuade young Muslims around the world to view the regional conflicts in various nations (Afghanistan, Syria, Iraq) as emergencies that require their immediate participation. As a result, tens of thousands of foreign fighters have left their homes to travel thousands of miles to kill and often die because they were convinced that their sacrifice is required.

Although situations (whether apparent or socially constructed) can be powerful, not everyone is equally likely to succumb to extremism. The great German-American social psychologist Kurt Lewin famously stated that behavior is determined by both *situation* and *personality*, and in Chapter 2 we have seen that people differ in their proclivity toward extremism. Some are more likely to exhibit extreme behavior than others. But the potential for motivational imbalance is part of our human nature beyond personality differences. And on the right occasion that potential might manifest in extremism.

EXTREMISM: DESTRUCTIVE AND CONSTRUCTIVE

Because in the popular lingo extremism is typically associated with violence, it has acquired a negative connotation. But the question of whether extremism is "bad" or "good" doesn't have a simple answer. The extremists make serious sacrifices for their particular passion. They often neglect basic needs such as proper nutrition and rest, as well as social needs such as the need to belong or be appreciated. Such neglect exacts a price, and the extremists often suffer as a result of their imbalanced life. Moreover, some types of extremism cause suffering to others. The extremists' friends and family may suffer from the alienation of their loved one, and violent extremists inflict untold suffering on the human targets of their aggression.

Most people would agree that violent extremism that indiscriminately kills innocents is unacceptable and criminal, and that its practitioners should be outlawed and punished. On September 20, 2001, that sentiment prompted President George W. Bush to announce the "global war on terror" (GWOT) and proclaim that it would not end until all terrorism worldwide was eradicated. Defeating all terrorism everywhere, like eradicating all crime, may be a utopian objective[2]— but we can agree that both are deplorable and should be fought.

What about other extremisms? Some, like addictions to drugs or alcohol, have few redeeming qualities. Both the society and the extremists themselves in moments of lucidity would concur that addiction is detrimental to wellbeing and should be treated. Other extremisms, however, might possess redeeming qualities that offset their costs. Hegel, the great German philosopher, said, "Nothing great in the world was accomplished without passion."[3] And passion at an uttermost levels is extremism. Would we like to have cooled down the passion of Van Gogh, of Marie Sklodowska-Curie, or that of Martin Luther King, Jr., or Jesus?

THE LAST TEMPTATION OF CHRIST

Martin Scorcese's 1988 film, The Last Temptation of Christ, presents a thought experiment of what it might have been like had Jesus turned to moderation. In a scene toward the end of the film, Jesus (played by Willem Dafoe) is dying in agony on the cross when a young, innocent-looking girl appears to him and claims to be his guardian angel. She tells him that, contrary to his belief, he is not the Messiah destined to save the world. Instead, he is God's beloved Son destined to be happy rather than suffer the torment of crucifixion. She proceeds to remove the nails from Jesus' bleeding wrists, brings him down off the cross, and takes him to Mary Magdalene, whom he marries. Jesus and Mary live a happy life, but when she abruptly dies, Jesus starts a family with Mary and Martha, the sisters of Lazarus. Then, as an elderly, ailing man on his deathbed, Jesus summons his former disciples to say goodbye.

The meeting doesn't turn out as expected, however. Judas, one of Jesus' closest intimates, upsets the grandeur of the occasion by revealing that the "guarding angel" that lured Jesus away from the cross is none other than Satan who tricked Jesus into believing he was not the Messiah. Mobilizing his last ounces of energy, the decrepit Jesus crawls back through the city of Jerusalem aglow with the fires of an anti-Roman rebellion, claws his way to the site of his crucifixion, and begs God to let him fulfill his purpose. Once again on the cross, having overcome the last temptation of living a quiet life of moderation. Scorcese's Jesus cries out: "It is accomplished!" and dies with a blissful smile on his face, a happy man and the extremist he was meant to be.

Scorcese resolved his thought experiment with the verdict of determinism: extremism is destiny. Not only that, but were it not for extremism, Scorcese's film implies, none of the great accomplishments of extremists would be possible. As psychologists, we cannot perform actual experiments to answer this question: it would be unethical to manipulate people into becoming extremists and compare their accomplishments with those who were guided toward moderation. Some questions are better suited for artistic than scientific exploration.

IS EXTREMISM WORTH IT?

Extremism certainly makes one stand out and be noticed. The sacrifices it entails also signal to the audience one's commitment to the cause, which may confer prestige and social worth on the extremist. A different question, however, is whether extremism is absolutely necessary for world-class attainments. Examples of outstanding achievers like Van Gogh, Sklodowska-Curie, or Gandhi might suggest that it is.

However, one kind of evidence against the necessity of extremism is the ability of moderate individuals to achieve extraordinary things. Amundsen, the South Pole explorer, in his moderation became the first person in history to reach the South Pole, and as a bonus saved his entire team and himself from freezing to death, which was the result of his rival's extremism. There are plenty of other examples of greatness that do not come with extremism—and so we can at least say that extremism is not a necessary condition for greatness. Ernest Hemingway, one of America's greatest writers, held strong passions for deep-sea fishing, big-game hunting, boxing, bullfighting, and war. Whereas early on he held himself to the "extreme" productivity standard of 1,000–2,000 words a day, the strain this induced brought about feelings of depression and deep melancholy. Consequently, he settled for a moderate goal of 500 words a day with much happier results.

Albert Einstein, among the greatest scientists who ever lived, had an active interest in philosophy and music, and if it wasn't for physics, he said, he would have been a concert violinist. He also had a vibrant social life, two wives and several mistresses. Picasso, one of

20th century greatest painters, too had a full and long life (he lived to 91), was deeply immersed in the society of his time; he was married twice and had four children.

Nor is extremism sufficient for great achievement: many more individuals fall victims of their extremism, losing their health, peace of mind, social connections, and sometimes their lives, than become beneficiaries of its fruits.

So, extremism and imbalance aren't exactly the prerequisites for greatness. In fact, one could wonder whether Van Gogh, who died by suicide at the age of 37, or Sklodowska-Curie, who suffered all her life deep bouts of depression and died of illness induced by radiation exposure, would not have had even more illustrious careers had their extremism not exerted its corrosive effects. It is possible they were extraordinarily successful despite their extremism, and not because of it.

These thoughts are highly relevant to our current age, replete with pressures that push people toward imbalanced lives driven by the desire to stand out. American children have had much of their play and free exploration time taken away, as they are pushed by their parents and the ambient culture to extreme academic and extracurricular efforts. Rather than discovering themselves and the world through playful experimentation, they are pressured to engage in just the "right," narrowly prescribed and closely supervised activities, and build just the right resumes to move along the academic trajectory to end up in prestigious colleges. Does that kind of goading to extreme effort so early in the child's life contribute to their future productivity, creativity, and accomplishment? It is difficult to answer this question empirically, or carry out rigorous research on this issue. What is beyond doubt, however, is that the competitive stresses take their toll, and that the mental health of American youth is in crisis. Even before the pandemic up to 1 in 5 US children aged 3–17 was having a mental, emotional, developmental, or behavioral disorder. And in a study conducted with 1,500 US parents nearly half of those interviewed (47%) reported that their teen is experiencing mental health challenges such as anxiety, depression, attention-deficit/hyperactivity disorder (ADHD), and autism spectrum disorder.[4] There are probably multiple causes to the mental crisis among American youth, including pandemic-induced isolation, over-exposure to the social media, unrelenting competition, and interpersonal comparison in academic, athletic, and social domains. They all combine to immense pressure, pushing American youngsters to the edge and eliciting extreme responses.

In sum, then, although some extremisms are clearly destructive and anti-social (those of the violent kind) and others are constructive and pro-social, they all exact a dear price to the extremists themselves and to others. Moreover, it isn't clear whether even the "positive," constructive extremisms are necessary or best suited to accomplish the worthy ends they are aimed at. It may be well to consider the ways of mitigating extremism.

MITIGATING EXTREMISM

What can be done to mitigate one's own or others' extremist tendencies? In what follows, we identify three strategies for doing so. These are our three injunctions of moderation, our three Ts: *Transcend*, *Tone down*, and *Tune in*.

Transcending. This mode of dealing with extremism involves transcending one's self-focus and shifting perspective to the outside world. Much of our tendency toward extremism stems from an excessive focus on one's own needs and prioritizing one's ego concerns, questing for social worth, significance, and the sense of mattering. In psychology, the juxtaposition to significance-driven egotism and self-aggrandizement is the state of *awe*, feelings of wonderment at the glory of nature, and the vastness of the universe.[5]

The significance–awe dilemma is poignantly illustrated by the story of Jesus' three temptations in the desert: as recorded in the Gospels (of Matthew, Mark, Luke, and John), Jesus was led into the wilderness by the Holy Spirit where he fasted for 40 days and nights. There he was tempted by the devil, who tried to divert him from his chosen path (of awe before the almighty) by evoking Jesus' human needs and dangling before him the allure of their satisfaction. The first temptation was to turn stones into bread—addressing Christ's hunger from fasting. The second temptation tested Jesus' need for control when the devil dared him to leap off the Temple roof, challenging God to save him from. The third, most trying temptation, evoked Jesus' needs for significance: the devil led Jesus to the top of a high mountain from which he could see all the kingdoms of the world, and said, "All this I will give you, if you will bow down and worship me." As the Gospels tell it, Jesus resisted all three temptations, thus transcending his self-centeredness and preserving his humility through the awesomeness of the divine.

We, mortals, can hardly hope for Jesus' divine connection. However, research finds that even the kind of awe derived from being in nature, spending a few minutes contemplating the sky or looking at trees or streams, can reduce political extremism.[6]

Highlighting the awe experience, shifting one's focus from one's self to the vast world of which one is but a minute and insignificant speck, is an effective way to mitigate extremist tendencies. Rather than striving to stand out and be counted, self-transcendence encourages one to feel in harmony with the universe, and experience calm unity and connection with other people and the environment.

Toning down. By toning down we mean reducing the intensity of one's desires, just as Buddhism recommends. Because extremism stems from the intense elevation of a given need, the desire to fulfill it rises accordingly. Attenuating such a desire should therefore curb extremism and encourage moderation.

Buddhism highlights the impermanence of all things. It therefore makes little sense to put too much stock on the fulfillment of one's needs, because things are fleeting, and fulfillment will not last. As Winston Churchill wisely noted, success isn't final and failure isn't fatal. This is why attachment (to people, ideals, or possessions, and significant emotional investment in desired outcomes) is, according to Buddhist teachings, the root of suffering.

Desire and aversion, representing such investments, are two of Buddhism's primary mental poisons responsible for much human suffering (the third is ignorance). Desire, the Buddhists observe, can lead to perfectionism, pride, low self-esteem, self-loathing, jealousy, and grief. A well-known Buddhist author, K. Sri Dhammananda, summarized this idea,

> If we don't get what we want, the feeling of emptiness continues. If we do get it, the desire is satisfied temporarily. But due to impermanence, the satisfaction fades, and new desires arise, creating an endless cycle... This continual search for satisfaction is the basis of mundane human life and leads to constant frustration.[7]

So how, according to Buddhist principles, should one fulfill essential needs and manage the desires they evoke? The Buddhist answer lies in the concept of the Middle Way: avoidance of extremes. Extremism leads to emotional highs and lows, fostering mental states that alternate between exuberance and agony. Moderation, on the other hand, results in quiet contentment, the ideal emotional state for a Buddhist.

Buddhism's practice of meditation helps loosen the grip of the mind on fears and desires. Meditation involves noticing one's thoughts and feelings (e.g. realizing that one is anxious, fearful, or ecstatic) rather than focusing on their content (e.g. "I failed the exam," "I will lose my job") or engaging with it (i.e. "I always fail," "I am a loser"). Meditation induces detachment from acute emotional experiences through the act of observation. This detachment allows the intensity of the emotional experience to subside (as all things tend to pass), reducing the tendency to prioritize it to the exclusion of other concerns, and mitigating extremism.

The influence of Buddhism is evident in contemporary psychotherapy approaches such as mindfulness-based stress reduction (MBSR), mindfulness-based cognitive therapy (MBCT), dialectical behavior therapy (DBT), and acceptance and commitment therapy (ACT). These therapies incorporate Buddhist practices of meditation and mindfulness, aiming to help individuals cultivate moderation and avoid extremism.

Interestingly, research suggests that mindfulness meditation impacts brain function. For example, studies indicate that mindfulness leads to decreased activation of the amygdala, a brain structure that controls responses to emotional events. This supports the idea that meditation reduces people's emotional investment in positive and negative outcomes. While novice meditators initially show increased responsiveness in brain areas responsible for cognitive control when exposed to emotionally charged images, experienced meditators exhibit reduced activity in those areas. Research on the impact of mindfulness meditation on brain structures and processes is a promising and expanding field in neuroscience, likely to provide new insights into how our brains can better handle emotional experiences and avoid extremism stemming from them.

TUNING IN

Extremism results from channeling most of one's mental energies into one focal need, and tuning out from nearly everything else. Such single-minded focus removes all constraints from behaviors aimed to satisfy this dominant need, creating a situation where in the name of that goal "anything goes," no matter the damage it causes. An important strategy of countering extremism is, therefore, refocusing on—or tuning in—to other, temporarily neglected concerns.

Multifinality. Making salient things that were originally neglected by the extremist does not mean abandoning the dominant concern around which extremism developed in the first place. Rather, it means finding ways and means for satisfying all of one's concerns. In psychology we call such multi-purpose activities multifinal, which means serving several different ends at the same time. Cell phones that have become an integral part of people's lives, are multifinal in a big way. Ostensibly means of communication, they also are search engines of information, purveyors of music, repositories of books, notebooks, and more.

Bringing extremists to moderation. A prominent example of the tuning in strategy of mitigating extremism are the various deradicalization programs aiming to turn terrorists into moderates. Basically, such programs bring detained members of a terror organization to consider aspects of their lives that were suppressed or put on hold during their term as militants and find ways to satisfy their cravings for meaning and significance (that motivated their joining the terror group in the first place) in ways that satisfied their alternative needs as well, for love, family, the actualization of their talents, etc.

Our research team had a unique opportunity to assess a deradicalization program for members of a violent terror organization, the Liberation Tigers of Tamil Eelam (LTTE), a vicious and well-organized group that waged a 30-year war against the Sinhalese majority on the island of Sri Lanka. In 2009, the Sri Lankan government launched a decisive campaign to defeat the LTTE. To do so, the Sri Lankan Minister of Defense and later president, Gotabaya Rajapaksa, doubled the size of the Sri Lankan army and carried out a merciless campaign that resulted in the deaths of approximately 20,000 militants, and at the end of which the LTTE was dismantled. Its leader, Velupillai Prabakharan, was killed, and the remaining 11,500 fighters surrendered to the Sri Lankan military. Initially, these surrendered fighters feared severe punishment. Instead, they were placed in a deradicalization program that offered educational, artistic, and vocational activities designed to help them abandon extremism and find meaning and significance in peaceful pursuits that would facilitate reintegration into mainstream Sri Lankan society.

The program emphasized respectful treatment of the inmates to build their sense of confidence and self-worth. The "beneficiaries" of the program, term used to avoid pejorative labels like "terrorists," "militants," or "detainees," were given freedom of movement within the large detention camp and freedom of religious practice (the Sinhalese are predominantly Buddhist, while the Tamils are Hindu). Military personnel overseeing the center were unarmed, though armed guards were stationed at the camp's perimeter. Additionally, successful and well-respected Tamil community members were recruited to work with the detainees, serving as role models and inspiring them to develop professional, social, and emotional skills for successful reintegration into the community.

Our team studied this process in-depth, administering surveys to the detainees at three points during their year-long program. We compared a sample of detainees who received the full program (comprising all courses and activities) with a control group that received a much more limited program. At the end of the year, those who received the full program were significantly less extreme and less supportive of violence against the Sinhalese than those in the control group. Thus, the program appeared to be successful. Even more interestingly, feelings of self-worth and personal significance were significantly higher among detainees who received the full deradicalization program compared to those in the control group. This difference in feelings of significance was responsible for the greater decline in support for violence among detainees exposed to the full program.[8]

Thus, by tuning in to the neglected aspects of their lives and finding multifinal means of addressing them, while also discovering meaning and significance in peaceful constructive pursuits, the detainees relinquished their extremism and embraced moderation.

Inviting extremism to tea. Extremism may not be as esoteric as we'd like to think, and it will likely become more common as our society's competitive individualism and comparison-inducing interconnectedness continue to grow. If we can't beat it, and don't want to join it, perhaps we can learn to live with it by "inviting extremism to tea," getting to know its hallmarks, and how to tame it. Because extremism is increasingly relevant to our lives, awareness of its workings and of ways of coping with its pressures can help navigate our everydays and lead to happier, more fulfilling lives.

The following true story recounts an instance of "taking extremism to tea." It is the story of Mohammad Farooq, a radicalized 28-year-old clinical support worker. On January 20, 2023, Farooq arrived at St James's Hospital in Leeds, UK, armed with two knives, an imitation firearm and a pressure cooker bomb double the size of that used in the 2013 Boston Marathon attack, which killed three and injured hundreds. Farooq's scheme was to trigger an evacuation via a bomb threat he texted to a nurse; this was intended to lure patients and staff into a deadly trap in which Farooq hoped to detonate his device in the middle of the huddled crowd, producing unthinkable casualties.

Things rarely go exactly as planned, however, and in this case it is quite fortunate that they didn't. The nurse Farooq texted happened to be off-duty, and did not see his message until later. As a back-up plan, he then decided to set off his homemade device in the hospital cafe. There he was spotted by the true hero of the story, a patient named Nathan Newby.

Mr Newby noted Farooq's visible distress and proceeded to approach him "to see if he was alright." It was Newby's calm and empathetic demeanor that encouraged Farooq to confide in him, and ultimately disclose his terrifying plan, conceived as a retribution against his colleagues who, on his account, had been bullying him. Despite Farooq's alarming story, Mr Newby maintained his composure and his empathetic attitude. He listened patiently to Farooq's grievances and managed to calm him down to the point of letting Newby to call emergency services, and allowing himself to be arrested.

The story has a happy ending. Farooq was convicted of preparing acts of terrorism at Sheffield Crown Court on Tuesday, July 2, 2024. Even though no actual tea was apparently involved, it was Mr Newby's serenity and humanity that allowed Farooq's inner turmoil to sedate, and his burning desire for revenge against his colleagues to simmer down. And an act of horrifying extremism was therefore averted.

IN SUMMARY

Extremism is characterized by several properties all emanating from the same source, the motivational imbalance between one's fundamental needs: (1) Extremism is rare in that relatively few people engage in extreme behaviors, (2) it involves sacrifices on the part of the extremists, (3) it is rational from the extremist's perspective in that it involves the pursuit of their utmost goal with what they see as the best means to that objective. And (4) it is salient and attention-grabbing because of its outstanding nature. The source of extremism from the psychological standpoint is putting all of one's mental and energetic resources into one dominant need and withdrawing them from all other concerns. Such motivational imbalance is a matter of degree; when it exceeds a given threshold, the individual is ready to do just about anything, no matter how costly or harmful, for this one dominant cause. Whereas some extremisms were associated with highly positive outcomes (great scientific discoveries, political progress, magnificent works of art) and other extremisms were associated with devastation and destruction (addiction, terrorism, wars), in nearly all cases, extremism exacts a serious personal price from those who succumb to it. Moreover, it isn't entirely clear that extremists' notable accomplishments necessitated their sacrifices, or would have been possible also through a more balanced goal pursuit.

In these times of growing worldwide tendencies toward extremism causing polarization and the fraying of societies it may be well to consider ways of reining in extremism. Psychology offers three major approaches to accomplishing this objective: transcending one's egotism and one's insatiable quest for significance; toning down the magnitudes of one's cravings; and tuning in to the panoply of all of one's needs rather than shutting them out in favor of one idée fixe.

These three ways of attenuating extremism, taking it to tea, as it were, can avoid the torments and agony extremists often suffer; in some cases too (those of ideological and/or violent extremism) ushering moderation may inspire harmony between people and nations making for a more peaceful, kinder, and gentler world.

NOTES

1 Kruglanski, A. W., & Orehek, E. (2009). Toward a relativity theory of rationality. *Social Cognition*, 27, 639–660. https://doi.org/10.1521/soco.2009.27.5.639

2 Kruglanski, A. W., & Fishman, S. (2006). The psychology of terrorism: Syndrome versus tool perspectives. *Terrorism and Political Violence, 18*, 193–215. https://doi.org/10.1080/09546550600570119

3 Goodreads. (n.d.). *Georg Wilhelm Friedrich Hegel quotes (Author of phenomenology of spirit)*. Goodreads. https://www.goodreads.com/author/quotes/6188 .Georg_Wilhelm_Friedrich_Hegel

4 Chilikova, K. (2023, October 8). The US youth mental health crisis demands a community response. *The Economist*. https://impact.economist .com/perspectives/health/us-youth-mental-health-crisis-demands-com- munity-response

5 Moskalenko, S., & Kruglanski, A. W. (2024). Significance-questing or awe- stricken: On two paradigms of meaning. In K. Fujita, N. Liberman, & A. Fishbach (Eds.), *The psychological quest for meaning*. Guilford.

6 Stancato, D. M., & Keltner, D. (2021). Awe, ideological conviction, and per- ceptions of ideological opponents. *Emotion, 21*(1), 61. https://doi.org/10 .1037/emo0000665

7 Sri, D. K. (1993). *What Buddhists believe* (p. 36). Buddhist Missionary Society.

8 Webber, D., Chernikova, M., Kruglanski, A. W., Gelfand, M. J., Hettiarachchi, M., Gunaratna, R., Lafreniere, M. A., & Belanger, J. J. (2017). Deradicalizing detained terrorists. *Political Psychology, 39*(3), 539–556. 10.1111/pops.12428

Printed in the United States
by Baker & Taylor Publisher Services